A HOPE FOR POETRY

A Hope for Poetry

By C. Day Lewis

Oxford: Basil Blackwell

1934

PRINTED IN GREAT BRITAIN
AT THE SHAKESPEARE HEAD PRESS
ST ALDATES OXFORD

To C. M. BOWRA

FOREWORD

THIS book is an examination of a section of post-war poetry. It is neither an apology nor a defence; truth is poetry's only defence, and true poetry can defend itself. The reader must look to it, and nowhere else, for its own vindication. The object of my book is to make the reader look — or look again — in a certain direction. It is based on the belief that some of the post-war writers, notably W. H. Auden and Stephen Spender, are true poets having more in common than mere contemporaneousness, and the belief that a discussion of their social and literary influences, their aims and their technique, may lead the reader to verify this for himself. I am not, therefore, writing primarily for the expert or the converted, though they may find some useful by-products here. Nor am I arranging another of those cheap excursions for the idle curious. It is a difficult country these poets have entered, and we need to have some of their spirit and all our wits about us if we are to follow them.

I have used the term 'post-war poets' to denote those who did not begin to write verse till after the war: I am conscious that there are young writers producing good work outside the particular field with which I am dealing here, and no belittlement is implied by their omission.

I have been compelled here and there to quote from my own poems. When I do so, it is because they offered the most convenient illustrations of given points, and with no reference to the title of this book.

C. D. L.

February, 1934.

A HOPE FOR POETRY

CHAPTER I

IN English poetry there have been several occasions on which the younger son, fretting against parental authority, weary of routine work on the home farm, suspecting too that the soil needs a rest, has packed his bag and set out for a far country. Rumours of his doings come to our ears: they are generally unfavourable, and always distorted, for they have had to pass across seas. He is flirting with foreign whores, we hear, or with ghosts: he has wasted his fortune: he has forgotten how to speak English: he has shamed his father: he has gone mad in the desert: he died some years ago. There is a great deal of indignation in the home town. Only his father smiles indulgently, feeling a secret pride, assured of the vigour of his seed. Then the younger son returns, not a broken prodigal, but healthy, wealthy and wise. He has many acres under cultivation over there, we find: he has money in the bank, strange tales to tell us, and some fine children already. We assure him that we had said all along he would make good, but we cannot help feeling a bit small.

A century and a half ago English poetry left those formal gardens brought to perfection by Dryden and Pope, where now their successors seemed able to raise only forced blooms and artificial flowers, and went into the wilderness for a change of air, a transfusion of blood. There Blake built a chapel to an unrecognized god, and Wordsworth heard on his mountain-sides the still small voice of gods almost forgotten. Coleridge went to sea with an ancient mariner and was made immortal on those uncharted waters, though he returned from them a ghost. The boy Keats, like Thomas the Rhymer, was rapt by a belle dame sans merci, and rode with her across the frontiers of fancy. We had many a hearty laugh at their antics, their wild-goose chases, but as the years went by we began to see that they had made the wilderness blossom like a rose. So it was roses, roses all the way

b

for a while: the full-blooded, frank romantic rose; till under the strain of constant crossings and variations it lost its scent. Yes, that desert is populous now. Where the first romantic poets staked out their claims, there are great cities, and many budding townships that follow their style of architecture. Tennyson, the master-builder of verse, is running up his monumental buildings, with one eye on Beauty and the other on Queen Victoria. But something has been happening. Little rifts and cracks are beginning to appear in the whole bland, ecclesiastical façade of Victorian England, and some of the more sensitive occupants are feeling the wind. There are tremors beneath our feet, and a great din of grouting fills our ears, through which we can dimly hear the voice of Matthew Arnold calling upon poetry to save our souls. At this interesting moment a Latin scholar, A. E. Housman, flinging round him a mantle of stoicism, broke out into a pure, unrivalled burst of song, the last lyric ecstasy we were to hear for many a long day; and as suddenly fell silent: while a young Jesuit, Gerard Manley Hopkins, slipped off unnoticed and took a train for an unknown destination.

Then came for poetry, in spite of Hardy and De la Mare, a period of very low vitality. The Georgian poets, a sadly pedestrian rabble, flocked along the roads their fathers had built, pointing out to each other the beauty spots and ostentatiously drinking small-beer in a desperate effort to prove their virility. The winds blew, the floods came: for a moment a few of them showed on the crest of the seventh great wave; then they were rolled under and nothing marks their graves. One only rode the whirlwind: Wilfrid Owen, killed on the Sambre canal, spoke above the barrage and the gas-cloud, saying to us, 'The poetry is in the pity.' When it was all over, it was left to an American, T. S. Eliot, to pick up some of the fragments of civilization, place them end to end, and on that crazy pavement walk precariously through the waste land.

Post-war poetry was born amongst the ruins. Its immediate ancestors are Hopkins, Owen and Eliot, the nature of whose

several influences I shall examine more closely in the sequel.
Other influences, of course, have been at work. As a poet, Eliot
has transmitted the power of the French Symbolist Movement:
as a critic, he has done much to popularize the seventeenth-
century metaphysicals & the Elizabethan dramatists: Donne, in
particular, is sympathetic to the post-war generation. Yeats, the
last in the aristocratic tradition of poets, remains the most ad-
mired of living writers: none of us can touch his later work, and
it is too personal in idiom, too insulated to allow an easy communication of its powers. He stands, a lesson to us in integrity,
demanding from us a complete subjection to the poetry that
occupies us, yet never asking of poetry more than lies within its
proper jurisdiction. Of prose-writers James Joyce stands alone
in the technical influence he has exerted, while the spiritual impact of D. H. Lawrence is at present almost equally remarkable,
though its effects are likely to be less lasting. On the whole,
however, that close connection between prose and poetry which,
as Eliot has justly pointed out, is vital to a healthy state of
literature, has not been achieved.

I have claimed Hopkins, Owen and Eliot as our immediate
ancestors. Before I attempt to expound this, it would be well to
examine the word 'ancestors.' I have used it deliberately, because the idea of ancestor-worship has developed for some of us
a strange potency. It expresses for us, in a word, the only possible patriotism, the one necessary link with the past, and the
meaning of tradition. Auden, who speaks naturally in parables,
makes the Airman of his book, *The Orators*, write in his Diary:

It wasn't till I was sixteen and a half that he (an uncle) invited
me to his flat. We had champagne for dinner. When I left I knew
who and what he was — my real ancestor.

That, in its context, seems to me one of the great moments of
the book. This feeling that each of us has some personal link
with the past, some natural or quasi-supernatural being from
whom we draw power and refreshment, someone with whom a

sudden recognition of kinship takes place, is of the first importance to us. It is not, I think, a poetical version of humanism. It
certainly is not a survival into our clouded day of patron saints
or guardian angels. Christianity may seem to have failed in its
task of civilizing religion, but we do not pretend to have found
here a substitute for religion or require that such a thing should
exist. We claim for these 'real ancestors' only this: that great
men, heroes, men who have seemed to live at a higher pressure
than the rest, can brim over into posterity. Their immortality is
not through lip-service and stone monuments, not in any act of
memory; is not external to us, but works in our minds, our
blood and our bones. This feeling has found its highest expression in Stephen Spender's poem. 'I think continually of those
who were truly great.' And it is one of Spender's greatest merits
that, when he tells us he thinks continually of those who were
truly great, we are in no doubt that he does do so.

> I think continually of those who were truly great.
> Who, from the womb, remembered the soul's history
> Through corridors of light where the hours are suns
> Endless and singing, whose lovely ambition
> Was that their lips, still touched with fire,
> Should tell of the Spirit clothed from head to foot in song.
> And who hoarded from the Spring branches
> The desires falling across their bodies like blossoms.
>
> What is precious is never to forget
> The essential delight of the blood drawn from ageless springs
> Breaking through rocks in worlds before our earth.
> Never to deny its pleasure in the morning simple light
> Nor its grave evening demand for love.
> Never to allow gradually the traffic to smother
> With noise and fog the flowering of the spirit.
>
> Near the sun, near the snow, in the highest fields,
> See how these names are fêted by the waving grass
> And by the streamers of white cloud
> And whispers of wind in the listening sky.

The names of those who in their lives fought for life.
Who wore at their hearts the fire's centre.
Born of the sun they travelled a short while towards the sun,
And left the vivid air signed with their honour.

There are certain obvious and superficial defects in this poem.
The transition from image to image is sometimes a little blurred,
and there is a tendency for the image sequences to be stretched
rather too far for coherence. But merit easily outweighs defect.
We are aware at once of that gravity and inward illumination —
passion glowing through a crystal sincerity —which makes the
best of Spender's verse so appealing. The Great War tore away
our youth from its roots. I see in this poem a successful attempt
to re-establish communication with the past, a minor miracle
of healing. And it takes the form of ancestor-worship. To re-
inforce this point I will quote part of a poem of my own:

> For those who had the power;
> Unhesitating, whether to kill or cure:
> Those who were not afraid
> To dam the estuary or start the forest fire:
> Whose hearts were filled
> With enthusiasm as with a constant wind
> That, lifting the fog, the pall of vision, unveiled
> Their own memorial, the stars: —
> There need be neither obituary nor wreath,
> Accomplices of death.
> These disappeared into the darkness ahead:
> Followers shall find
> Them walking larger than legends in that virgin land;
> Their spirit shall be blowing out of the sunrise,
> Their veins our rivers, their bones our bread.

So it is with a poet's real ancestors. They disappear into the
darkness ahead, and he who follows finds that they are not
merely the geographers but in a sense the creators of his poetical
world.

CHAPTER II

HOPKINS, Owen and Eliot are recent examples of younger sons who could not stay at home. They have little else apparently in common: whereas the Muse of Eliot would be hard put to it to say which of a dozen or so lovers was the real father, Hopkins as a poet seems to have entered the world by a kind of partheno-genesis. The author of such lines as these —

> I caught this morning morning's minion, king —
> Dom of daylight's Dauphin, dapple-dawn-drawn Falcon, in
>   his riding.

or this —

> Or to-fro tender tram beams truckle at the cye —

is difficult to connect with anything in the past. Attempts have been made to trace his derivation back to Milton. Except for Hopkins's own statement that Milton's counterpoint rhythm, particularly as used in the choruses of *Samson Agonistes*, is apt to become identical with the 'sprung rhythm' which Hopkins himself used, I can see no warrant for such a derivation. The nearest approach to his verse texture I can find is in the Greek choruses, more especially those of Æschylus: we may note in his work something of the same fluidity of line, the same architectural massiveness and decorated verbal accumulation.

Leaving aside verse-texture, and considering what I must call, rather vaguely, poetic merit, I find eminent in Hopkins that quality which made Shakespeare supreme. Eliot, in a recent work, has expressed it as follows: 'The re-creation of word and image which happens fitfully in the poetry of such a poet as Coleridge happens almost incessantly with Shakespeare. Again and again, in his use of a word, he will give a new meaning or extract a latent one. . . .' That 're-creation of word and image' is the last secret of poetic technique, and the extent to which Hopkins achieved it may be gauged by the excerpts printed below:

the sensitive reader may discover in them, also, something of the quality and 'feel' of Shakespeare's own poetry.

> Look at the stars! look, look up at the skies!
>   O look at all the fire-folk sitting in the air!
>   The bright boroughs, the circle-citadels there! . . .

(Juliet might be speaking there.)

> As a dare-gale skylark scanted in a dull cage . . .

>   are you that liar
>   And, cast by conscience out, spendsavour salt?

But, for all this, Hopkins remains without affinities. Poets may be divided into two classes; those who assimilate a number of influences and construct an original speech from them, and those whose voice seems to come out of the blue, reminding us of nothing we have heard before. Amongst the younger present-day writers, Auden is obviously of this first class, Spender of the second. Eliot's poetry is an extreme example of the former: Lawrence's, of the latter. These categories carry no implication of poetic merit. The integration of many influences into an individual voice requires a true poet: but he is not, because of this process, to be called a greater or a lesser poet than he whose work has not undergone the process. Nor does the second category imply an absence of poetical self-consciousness: that is to say, one may have a close acquaintance with other poets, dead and living, yet remain as a poet almost untouched by them. The sophisticated critic may be the naïf poet, as witness A. E. Housman. It is possible that Housman's own definition of the class of things to which poetry belongs may be true only for the naïf poet: 'I should call it a secretion: whether a natural secretion, like turpentine in the fir, or a morbid secretion, like the pearl in the oyster': while in the sophisticated, assimilative poet more complex motive powers are at work. We do not suppose, of course, that any poet can remain entirely unaffected by the work of other poets; or that anyone can produce poetry by however skilful a blending of the best ingredients. The naïf poet, too, may sometimes write sophisticated poetry, or even turn into a sophisticated poet—it seems increasingly difficult, indeed, for him to avoid doing so. But it is possible to put the bulk of a poet's work over a number of years into one class or the other.

Though one or two of Hopkins's mature poems come into the first class ('The Blessed Virgin compared to the Air we Breathe,' for instance, which, except for a line here and there, might have been written by one of the metaphysical school), he is predominantly what I have called a 'naïf' poet. (Since writing this section, I have discovered in one of Hopkins's letters the following passage: 'The effect of studying masterpieces is to make me admire and do otherwise . . .') It is, therefore, all the more remarkable to find him exerting such an influence on modern verse; for poets of this type do not belong to any 'school' of poetry and are apt not to found one. We admire Blake or Housman from a distance: any closer approach to their technique would lead us into pastiche. This is, perhaps, because their technique springs more immediately and purely from their experience than is the case with the 'sophisticated' writer. Up to a point this is true of Hopkins's also: one is frequently coming across undigested fragments of his style imbedded in post-war verse. But he has had a much more real influence than this mere bequeathing of echoes: and it is due, I think, to the fact that, unlike most naïf poets, he was a technical innovator. Such poets (Blake, Housman, Emily Dickinson) are usually content to work within conventional forms: their dæmon does the rest. It may seem contradictory to assert that a technical innovator can be a naïf poet, but I do not believe it is necessarily so. I should even go so far as to call Hopkins an unconscious revolutionary: in other words, his innovations are not due to a deliberate rebelling against the conventional technique of the time, as were those of Wordsworth, but spring from a kind of innocent experimenting with words, as a child of genius might invent a new style of architecture while playing with bricks.

One of Hopkins's most striking innovations is his frequent use of what he calls 'sprung rhythm.' It is not perhaps quite accurate to term it an innovation, for it approximates to the rhythm of *Piers Plowman* and the old nursery rhymes. But to all intents and purposes it is revolutionary. Wordsworth aimed at simplifying poetry, bringing it nearer to common speech: he effected this by a radical change in the use of words, not by radical changes in prosody. Hopkins was not working on any such theory of communication, but he produced in fact a result the opposite of Wordsworth: by him the language of poetry was removed almost as far as possible from ordinary language—it becomes incantation again; while his prosody swings to the other extreme, for it is based on the rhythm of common speech. We find in post-war poetry a tendency to combine these two results, to use common speech rhythms together with a mixture of simplified, superficially un-'poetical' language and highly poetical incantatory language.

Till Hopkins, almost all English verse since Langland had been written in metres divisible into feet of two or three syllables, iambic or dactylic-anapæstic in effect. It is therefore syllabically quantitative[1] verse. Any variations, such as the substitution of trochee for iamb, had been variations on a metre of not less than two syllables per foot, and the beat—except in a few strictly dactylic poems, 'Take her up tenderly'—had the effect of coming on the last syllable of the foot. Sprung rhythm differs from this quantitative metre in the following ways. It is based on one syllable stressed in each foot: this syllable may stand alone in its foot or it may be accompanied by a number of unstressed syllables, usually not more than four. Thus lines such as these—

Hígh there, how he húng upon the réin of a wímpling wíng.
No wónder of it: shéer plód makes plóugh down síllion . . .

would have the same value, five stresses, as

. . . When yoú shall thése unlúcky deéds reláte . . .

[1] Quantitative is used here in the sense of a given number of syllables per foot, not in the classical sense.

The stress, where there is more than one syllable in the foot, comes as a rule on its first syllable: but a uniformly trochaic-dactylic effect is avoided by the use of what Hopkins called 'out-rides,' unstressed syllables occasionally placed before the stressed ones at the beginning of the foot. Thus in his metres the stress is the foundation, whereas in English verse as a whole, quantity —i.e. two or three syllables to a foot—is the foundation. And since stress is the basis of common speech rhythm, we may say that this sprung rhythm approximates to the rhythm of common speech.

In its favour as a poetical instrument we can put forward a greater freedom for rhythmical effects than is afforded by sylla-bically-quantitative metre with all its possible licences. No such lively representation of the hover and swoop of a kestrel could be achieved within the limits of the latter as we find in the first of the lines quoted above. And in the second, the heavy deter-mination of 'sheer plod,' with its successive stresses accentuated by the three unstressed syllables before them, is again an effect which could not be procured within a conventional metre. On the other hand, the metrical foundation of sprung rhythm is so shifting and elastic that in employing it we are almost bound to lose that most desirable of rhythmical effects, the counterpoint of the line spoken according to the natural rhythm of the words working in contrast to the strict beat of the metre. As for in-stance we hear the metrical beat in—

> . . . Cancél and téar to piéces thát great bónd
> Which kéeps me pále! Light thíckens, ánd the crów . . .

counterpointed by the speech rhythm—

> Cáncel and teár to piéces that greát bónd
> Which kéeps me pále! Líght thíckens and the crów . . .

Another objection to sprung rhythm as used by Hopkins is that it often does not conform closely enough to common speech rhythm: we find ourselves compelled to run over a number of heavy syllables, which would certainly be stressed in ordinary speech, before we come to the intended stress. The intended stress, indeed, is often difficult to find. It is comparatively seldom that a series of consecutive lines speak themselves as easily as the first verse of his great poem 'The Wreck of the Deutschland.'

> Thóu mástering me
> Gód! gíver of breáth and bréad:
> Wórld's stránd, swáy of the séa
> Lórd of líving and déad;
> Thou hast boúnd bónes and veíns in me, fástened me flésh
> And áfter it álmost unmáde, whát with dréad
> Thy doíng: and dóst thou toúch me afrésh?
> Over agáin I feél thy fínger and fínd thée.

And even here, though the number of stresses is indicated by the setting of the lines, we are compelled once or twice to verify them from other verses.

Less questionably successful than Hopkins's use of sprung rhythm is his use of alliteration and internal assonance. He employs both constantly, yet, like all successful technical tricks, they are indistinguishable from the pattern which they help to create. These devices are seen to best advantage in 'The Leaden Echo and the Golden Echo,' a poem which is coupled in my mind with Tennyson's 'Ballad of the Revenge' as representing the most remarkable technical achievement of Victorian poetry. It begins—

> How to keep—is there any any, is there none such,
>   nowhere known some, bow or brooch or braid or brace,
>   lace, latch or catch or key to keep
> Back Beauty, keep it, beauty, beauty, beauty, . . .
>   from vanishing away? . . .

Notice how cunningly alliteration and assonance are contrived to modulate from one vowel key into another. Yet there is nothing forced, no flavour of artifice. The poem must be read aloud, and with an unprejudiced intellect, for it is a sustained sensual rhapsody; something for which our acquaintance with civilized poetry leaves us unprepared. It is the measure of Hopkins's poetical stature that, though a man of great intellectual ability, he was capable of writing this kind of rhapsody without ever degenerating into rhetoric.

> . . . Only not within seeing of the sun,
> Not within the singeing of the strong sun,
> Tall sun's tingeing, or treacherous the tainting of the
>   earth' sair . . .

Alliteration, internal assonance and repetition are the chief instruments used by Hopkins in creating a poetry of rare concentration: we find them all used, though not at such high frequency, in post-war verse. The flight of his imagination is very swift: the following of it often a breathless business. What obscurity we may find when first we read him is due, not to a clouded imagination or an unsettled intellect, but to his lightning dashes from image to image, so quick that we are unable at first to perceive the points of contact. He is a true revolutionary poet, for his imagination was always breaking up and melting down the inherited forms of language, fusing them into new possibilities, hammering them into new shapes. His intense faith and his violent spiritual agonies are experiences which few of us to-day—happily or unhappily—are able to share: they caused some of his most magnificent poems: with one of these, the greatest poem to my mind that he ever wrote, we may salute him and take our leave.

> No worst, there is none. Pitched past pitch of grief,
> More pangs will, schooled at forepangs, wilder wring.
> Comforter, where, where is your comforting?
> Mary, mother of us, where is your relief?
> My cries heave, herds-long; huddle in a main, a chief
> Woe, world-sorrow; on an age-old anvil wince and sing—
> Then lull, then leave off. Fury had shrieked, 'No lingering! Let me be fell: force I must be brief.'

O the mind, mind has mountains: cliffs of fall
Frightful, sheer, no-man-fathomed. Hold them cheap
May who ne'er hung there. Nor does long our small
Durance deal with that steep or deep. Here! creep,
Wretch, under a comfort serves in a whirlwind: all
Life death does end and each day dies with sleep.

CHAPTER III

GERARD MANLEY HOPKINS died young in the year 1889. His poems were not published till 1918, the year in which Wilfrid Owen was killed. Hopkins would have been a poet under any circumstances: Owen, I am inclined to think, was made a poet by the war. The notes which he set down for a preface to his poems give the clue to his identity.

This book is not about heroes. English poetry is not yet fit to speak of them. Nor is it about deeds or lands, nor anything about glory, honour, dominion or power,
except War.
Above all, this book is not concerned with Poetry.
The subject of it is War, and the pity of War.
The Poetry is in the pity.
Yet these elegies are not to this generation,
This is in no sense consolatory.
They may be to the next.
All the poet can do to-day is to warn.
That is why the true Poets must be truthful.

This noble, fragmentary message reached the next generation, as he hoped, and meant more to them than perhaps he ever had expected. We must be careful not to misunderstand him, though. When he says that his book 'is not concerned with Poetry,' he is not simply expressing what most artists feel at times, particularly at times of great external crisis—a sense of the ineffectiveness and isolation of their own form of life. Nor does he imply that poetry can ever be concerned with itself to any advantage. He is saying, I think, that there are times when the poet's allegiance must be divided: when his duty towards his neighbour ceases to be necessarily identical with his duty towards his god, Poetry, the former acquiring temporarily a relatively enlarged significance in his mind. In other words, circumstances may force the poet unwillingly to take up the posi-

tion of prophet—'all the poet can do to-day is to warn.' Again,
when he says, 'That is why the true Poets must be truthful,' he is
not suggesting that there are times when true Poets are allowed
to tell lies. There is poetical truth, and there is common honesty;
they are very distant relations: Owen's plea was that the crisis
should bring them together, that the greater—poetical truth—
should temporarily put itself under the command of the lesser.
Owen commends himself to post-war poets largely because they
feel themselves to be in the same predicament; they feel the same
lack of a stable background against which the dance of words
may stand out plainly, the same distrust and horror of the unnatural forms into which life for the majority of people is being
forced. They know in their hearts exactly what Owen meant
when he said 'the poetry is in the pity.'

> Move him into the sun—
> Gently its touch awoke him once,
> At home, whispering of fields unsown.
> Always it woke him, even in France,
> Until this morning and this snow.
> If anything might rouse him now
> The kind old sun will know.

> Think how it wakes the seeds—
> Woke, once, the clays of a cold star.
> Are limbs so dear-achieved, are sides
> Full-nerved—still warm—too hard to stir?
> Was it for this the clay grew tall?
> O what made fatuous sunbeams toil
> To break earth's sleep at all?

It is difficult to call this anything but a perfect poem. Poetical
truth becoming here, as in almost all his poems, the servant of
common honesty—of Owen's determination to tell the factual,
un-'poetical' truth, so far from being cramped and degraded, is
enlarged and glorified. Owen had mastered that easy, almost
conversational kind of verse at which many of the Georgian

poets were aiming, in their reaction away from the laborious magniloquence of the 'Nineties': unlike them, he never seems to lose dignity in the process; he speaks as one having authority, never condescending to language or adopting the hail-fellow-well-met tones of the poet who has a craving to be 'understood.' The first verse of the poem quoted above is an object lesson in the simplicity that never was paucity: in the second, engined with pity and indignation, the poetry leaves the ground and ascends into heaven, culminating on a line, 'Was it for this the clay grew tall?' which would stand out from the work of any but the greatest poets.

One of the traditional tests of a poet is the number of out-standing, memorable lines he has written: this test Owen passes triumphantly. The lines of his which stick most in our memory can be divided into two types. The first of these is highly 'poeti-cal,' in the grand manner, reminding us of Keats — a poet with whom Owen had a great deal more in common than an early death. It is exemplified in such lines as —

> ... Whatever shares
> The eternal reciprocity of tears.

> ... Whose world is but the trembling of a flare,
> And heaven but as the highway for a shell. ...

> ... Mine ancient scars shall not be glorified
> Nor my titanic tears the seas be dried.

The second type is restrained, often witty in the seventeenth-century sense, always ironical: it works through a kind of under-statement which recalls to us at once the grim and conscious irony of those who knew that 'their feet had come to the end of the world.' We find it perpetually recurring in his work. He is writing of a draft entraining for the front —

> Dull porters watched them, and a casual tramp
> Stood staring hard,
> *Sorry to miss them from the upland camp.* ...

of a disabled soldier ('there was an artist silly for his face'), help-
less in a wheeled chair —

> ... Now he is old; his back will never brace;
> *He's lost his colour very far from here,*
> Poured it down shell-holes till the veins ran dry. ...

Or, in his poem 'Greater Love,' the lines —

> Heart, you were never hot,
> Nor large, nor full like hearts made great with shot; ...

These deliberate, intense under-statements — the brave man's
only answer to a hell which no epic words could express — affect
me as being both more poignant and more rich with poetic
promise than anything else that has been done during this century. Owen was not a technical revolutionary: his one innovation is the constant use of the alliterative assonance as an end
rhyme — (mystery, mastery; killed, cold). But he was a true revolutionary poet, opening up new fields of sensitiveness for his
successors. If he had lived there is no knowing what his promise
might have achieved; he would have found, active in different
guises, the cant, the oppression, the sufferings and courage
which had challenged his powers during the war. As it is, his
unsentimental pity, his savage and sacred indignation are the
best of our inheritance, and it is for his heirs to see that they are
not wasted.

c

CHAPTER IV

WHEN we turn from Owen's work to Eliot's we turn from irony to cynicism, from anger to exasperation, from wounds to nerves, from the love of living to the will to die. It is very much to Eliot's credit as a poet that he detected this death-will in western civilization before it rose to the surface in the disillusionment of the later war years. The death-will, some of whose many variations were soon to be recorded by D. H. Lawrence and W. H. Auden, appears as the motif of Eliot's 'Love Song of J. Alfred Prufrock,' first published in 1914. This poem, the most successful he has written, is both an easy introduction to the new verse technique and also a very instructive entry in the case-history of poetic feeling. We have seen how Hopkins's work was apt to be rendered obscure by the rapid transit of the sense from image to image: with him the process is a naïf one due to the high-frequency of the poetic current in him and to the intrinsically poetical quality of his thought. With Eliot it becomes, I think, a conscious process, a deliberate way of writing. Let us take an example. Prufrock is a middle-aged man—(it is generally accepted that Eliot as a poet was born middle-aged, and has not been getting any younger since); he is contemplating an appeal for sympathy to a fashionable woman, a proposal of marriage perhaps. He says—

> ... And should I then presume?
> And how should I begin?
>
> *   *   *   *   *
>
> Shall I say, I have gone at dusk through narrow streets
> And watched the smoke that rises from the pipes
> Of lonely men in shirt-sleeves, leaning out of windows? ...
>
> I should have been a pair of ragged claws
> Scuttling across the floors of silent seas.

The reader, unaccustomed to the total absence of logical continuity, is at first inclined to irritation. What have crabs and men

in shirt-sleeves to do with a middle-aged man debating a proposal of marriage? Let him not overheat his intellectual bearings
in an attempt to 'think out' the connections: the only entry into
the position is an emotional one. If he will allow the images to
cohabit in his mind for a little, he will find that a contact is made,
a spark thrown off which illuminates the whole situation. He
begins to notice the roundabout, diffident appeal for pity in the
image of lonely men smoking at windows: no abstract invocation to loneliness, but a single deliberately banal picture of it.
And then Mr Prufrock's musing mind switches suddenly off to
his own inferiority, his timidity, his incompetence: suppose he
were rejected; he would want to sink through the floor for hu-
miliation—to be 'scuttling across the floors of silent seas,' safe
under fathoms of water from these terrible human contacts and
emotional situations.

This deliberate use of what we may call emotional sequence is
one of the two efficient causes of the 'obscurity' of post-war
poetry. It is, in the first place, due to the influence of the French
symbolist school—especially of Rimbaud, Laforgue, Valéry: for
a discussion of this influence, the reader is referred to Edmund
Wilson's *Axel's Castle*, a book which may be coupled with some
of Eliot's own essays as representing the best of twentieth-
century literary criticism. It seems also to have grown up with
the advance of film technique, and may well have been influenced
by it. Just as a film director will use a series of superficially
unconnected 'shots' to express an emotional state or to carry
the mind from one dramatic point to another, so the poet will
employ a series of superficially unconnected images. I have
known intelligent people, who rarely go to the cinema, completely incapable of following the plot of a film in which this
technique was employed. Similarly, with post-war verse, the intelligent but untutored reader is apt to admit himself quite
baffled at the start: at the same time he is often interested and excited by individual images, and feels that, if only he had one
clue, he would be able to make his way quite easily through the

labyrinth. The object of this book being largely to persuade the prospective reader, and not to freeze him with assumptions of his mental inadequacy, I hope later to indicate some general clues which may be of assistance. He may feel reassured to know that poets are doing their best now to bridge the gulf from their side, and he does not need to be told that true poetry, however simple it may appear on the surface, accumulates meaning every time it is read.

We may find another parallel to this emotional sequence in empirical psychology. One of the psychologist's methods of exploring the dark interior is that of 'free association': a list of words is spoken to the subject, to each of which he answers the first word that comes into his head. This has always been, up to a point, the way poetry comes to be written: the poet 'has an idea,' and in the course of contemplating it he draws up from his subconscious a string of associated ideas and images. But there are two important differences which affect the poet and the reader to-day. In the first place, the poet is almost bound to have accepted the psychological hypothesis of the unconscious, and is therefore bound to be partly aware of the process of poetic creation. This self-consciousness, whether it is a genuine insight into the workings of his own mind or only a false explanation of them, is a source of grave embarrassment to him. Modern poets have tended to dealing with this embarrassment by a kind of ju-jitsu trick; they give way to free association, using their adversary's own strength to overcome him: whereas poets till recently have fought the stream from the unconscious by direct methods, so to speak, imposing their personality upon it, dividing its forces and tieing them up together with logical connections. The former process makes things difficult for the reader, because his associations with any given idea or image are probably different from those of the poet, and he is likely to feel as puzzled and uncomfortable as if he was listening to someone talking in their sleep.

Eliot is the best known exponent of this use of free associa-

tion in verse; in prose, James Joyce. There can be no doubt that
the latter has enormously influenced modern poets by his constant and successful employment of it. Take, for instance, the
opening lines of Eliot's 'Waste Land' —

> April is the cruellest month, breeding
> Lilacs out of the dead land, mixing
> Memory and desire, stirring
> Dull roots with spring rain.
> Winter kept us warm, covering
> Earth in forgetful snow, feeding
> A little life with dried tubers.
> Summer surprised us, coming over the Starnbergsee
> With a shower of rain; we stopped in the colonnade,
> And went on in sunlight, into the Hofgarten,
> And drank coffee, and talked for an hour.
> Bin gar keine Russin, stamm' aus Litauen, echt deutsch.
> And when we were children, staying at the archduke's,
> My cousins, he took me out on a sled,
> And I was frightened. He said, Marie,
> Marie, hold on tight. And down we went.
> In the mountains, there you feel free,
> I read much of the night, and go south in the winter. . . .

There is a perfect example of free association, deliberately
used by the poet to recreate a mood, 'mixing memory and desire.' I am at the moment concerned only with the facts: the
reader has not, I hope, been given to understand that this association is claimed as the only possible way of writing poetry to-
day or that the passage quoted above is necessarily claimed as
good poetry. He is probably in no danger of falling into the
error, common among modern would-be revolutionary verse-
writers, of assuming that free-association must inevitably produce poetry: it produces, in actual fact, little more than auto-
matic writing, unless it has passed through the usual poetic processes. Free association, then, or emotional sequence does not

make poetry: it conditions the form which poetry will take. The substitution of emotional for logical sequence, in so far as it is prevalent in post-war verse, may finally be classed as one of the manifestations of that general distrust of logic and dethroning of reason brought about by the Great War and formulated into a creed by D. H. Lawrence.

Eliot first came into prominence with the publication of 'The Waste Land.' This poem called forth floods of abuse and storms of intellectual snobbery: it provided the reactionary with something they could really get their teeth into, and the fake-progressives with a new fashion. It does not to my mind contain his best poetry: for that, I would direct the reader to 'Prufrock,' 'Gerontion,' one or two of his later poems—in particular, 'Animula,' and to such lines as—

> Eyes I dare not meet in dreams
> In death's dream kingdom
> These do not appear:
> There, the eyes are
> Sunlight on a broken column
> There, is a tree swinging
> And voices are
> In the wind's singing
> More distant and more solemn
> Than a fading star.

But the fact remains that, for good or ill, 'The Waste Land' has had a greater influence on present-day verse than the rest of Eliot's work and probably a greater one than any other poetry of the century. This is due largely to its subject matter—more so, perhaps, than to the novelties of its technique. I. A. Richards, who gives a terribly inflated value to the poem, says that it effects 'a complete severance between poetry and all beliefs,' an example of criticism at its most vicious. One can neither write nor exist completely severed from all beliefs, and the beliefs which a writer holds or against which he is reacting are bound to affect his writing. It is always dangerous and impertinent to commend a poem for anything but its poetry: however, I am compelled to say that 'The Waste Land' seems to me chiefly important as a social document. It gives an authentic impression of the mentality of educated people in the psychological slump that took place immediately after the war. It makes us aware of the nervous exhaustion, the mental disintegration, the exaggerated self-consciousness, the boredom, the pathetic gropings after the fragments of a shattered faith—all those symptoms of the psychic disease which ravaged Europe as mercilessly as the Spanish influenza. But in doing so it enlarged our conception of the field of poetic activity: as Eliot himself has said; 'the essential advantage for a poet is not, to have a beautiful world with which to deal; it is to be able to see beneath both beauty and ugliness; to see the boredom, and the horror, and the glory.'

Eliot's editors have been so occupied with extracting meanings from 'The Waste Land' that they have given comparatively little attention to 'Prufrock.' Otherwise they could not have failed to perceive the sinister nature of the allegory it contains. In the figure of Mr Prufrock, middle-aged, urbane, by turns romantic and disillusioned, capable of no more serious satire than a little rueful laughter at himself, we may see the modern poet, T. S. Eliot: the lady in the case, for whom he wonders 'Do I dare disturb the universe?', who (he is afraid) 'settling a pillow by her head, should say: "That is not what I meant at all; that is not it at all," ' is the sophisticated intelligentsia of his day. Mr Prufrock, at any rate, did make his proposal and was accepted. The marriage was a fashionable event: Mr Prufrock fitted in very well with his wife's social circle, and was quite the rage. He learnt their allusive language, their private jokes, their nervous gaiety. He became a leader of fashion. Then, to the visible embarrassment of his young associates, he suddenly tired of it all and joined the Anglo-Catholic persuasion: leadership of fashion was too much for him, for he was really an honest and a sensitive man, and he had found that you can pay too high a price for the possession of someone who 'understands' you. We see Mr Prufrock now, like most converts, meticulous over points of ritual, very severe and aloof in tone, repenting profusely for a viciousness that had never, may be, broken the bounds of phantasy. We may prefer the old unregenerate Prufrock: we will certainly regret the disappearance of that humour which was perhaps his chief asset: but we have to admit that he was justified in trying to clear right out of the racket.

CHAPTER V

PRUFROCK was a youngest son, and his marriage to Intelligentsia was, if not a withdrawal into the desert, at least a departure from his paternal home. While his elder brothers remained in the country or the cloister, Prufrock, like Dick Whittington, had come to town. His brothers, it is true, had sometimes been in town for visits or to transact a little business; but they had never stayed long and always hurried back as quickly as they could, dazed by the traffic or declaiming against the horrors of the place. Prufrock was the first to be at home there. The date of his taking up residence marks the beginning of a new stage in English poetic development: from that date a poetry began which was to draw its nourishment to a far greater extent from town civilization.

Unfortunately, Prufrock, as we have seen, became posh. And this did not do his children any good: they were irritated at being flattered for their father's virtues, and they did not care for basking in the arc-light of his publicity. There is little wonder that, in consequence, although they retained their respect for him and certain of his characteristics and mannerisms, they began to make up a private language of their own in self-defence, to become hearty, to play practical jokes, to hob-nob with social revolutionaries, and in general to assert their individuality. Before long they were highly disconcerted to find that they too had become posh. At this point the joke had clearly gone too far; and we may return to plain speaking.

There are superficial signs in the air at present of a boom in poetry: that they are only superficial and probably misleading I shall soon attempt to show. This boom has been connected in certain quarters with the names of Auden, Spender and myself. While it is gratifying, it is difficult at first to understand to what we may attribute this honour. Let us get it quite clear at the start. There is no living poet in English who has proved himself to be of the stature of Yeats: nor can I see any post-war poetry

which exhibits the triumph of personality that we find in the
poems of Hardy; there is little even that shows a technical vir-
tuosity equivalent to that of De la Mare. If we compare Mrs
Monro's anthology of 'Recent Poetry' with one of the Georgian
anthologies, we cannot assert that the general level of technique
is noticeably higher in the former. On the other hand, there does
seem to be an increase in what we may call vitality. And it is this
increased vitality which, I believe, has misled critics into positing
a poetic revival. The vigour, the 'optimism,' the revolutionary
fervour which undoubtedly are present in post-war poetry may
only be reflections of the mood of a society recovering from the
war. A poet is nothing if not sensitive to his environment: when
he feels all round him the blood beginning to circulate again and
the heart beating more strongly, it will be strange if this does
not communicate itself to his verse. We are not here concerned
with the question whether this recrudescence of energy that has
communicated itself to verse is the death throes of a social order
or the birth-pangs of a new one; or both; or neither, but just
simple convalescence. But it is important that we distinguish
between borrowed, adventitious energy in verse, and its natural
energy. To make good poetry there may be a vigour derived
from the poet's social environment, but there must be a different
and superior energy generated within the poem itself. Consider
the following three extracts from young living writers: in A I
find adventitious energy only; in B natural energy only; in C
natural plus adventitious energy.

A

            —leave, quickly leave
The empty acres and the splintered trunks,
Shoulder the household gods and take the train
Eastward to land where scattered grain gives root,
Quickly before the sentries take their aim
Lynx-eyed along the frontier, at the stations,
Before they post you TRAITOR on the walls,
Plant spies in ports, and wire the Flying Squad.
                                   (John Lehmann.)

B

More beautiful and soft than any moth
With burring furred antennae feeling its huge path
Through dusk, the air-liner with shut-off engines
Glides over suburbs and the sleeves set trailing tall
To point the wind. Gently, broadly, she falls
Scarcely disturbing charted currents of air.

(Stephen Spender.)

C

Which of you waking early and watching daybreak
Will not hasten in heart, handsome, aware of wonder
At light unleashed, advancing, a leader of movement,
Breaking like surf on turf on road and roof,
Or chasing shadow on downs like whippet racing,
Then stilled against stone, halting at eyelash barrier,
Enforcing in face a profile, marks of misuse,
Beating impatient and importunate on boudoir shutters
Where the old life is not up yet, with rays
Exploring through rotting floor and dismantled mill—
The old life never to be born again?   (W. H. Auden.)

I have deliberately chosen B in order to demonstrate the difference between the use of contemporary images objectively, where the poem does not receive through them extraneous energy from the social life of which these images are details; and the use of contemporary imagery, as in C, where to the intrinsic energy of the poem is added a social energy working through contemporary images so integrated with the poem as to release into it the external life they represent. When adventitious as well as natural energy is found in a poem, we shall incidentally find that very often a moral judgment also results.

The extracts printed above should give the reader some sense of both the false and the genuine vitality to be discovered in post-war verse. I have said that this increase of vitality has misled critics into postulating a poetic revival: in so far as this means a revival of poetry, we now realize that the statement must be qualified; an increase in the natural energy of poetry obviously does imply a poetic revival; it is only a failure to dis-

criminate between natural and borrowed energy which can mis-
lead. But I had also in mind the frequent use of the term 'poetical
revival' to connote an increased interest in poetry: and in this
sense one can feel very much less confidence in the critics' judgment.

What are the signs? One or two conservative publishers are
launching out series of modern verse: there is something of a
run on anthologies; medals are to be given to young hopefuls.
But it is difficult not to suspect that renewal of interest in poetry
proceeds largely from an interest in the social connections to be
found in much 'left-wing' work; that it is the communist or
fascist tendencies, the up-to-dateness of the imagery, the preoccupation with specifically modern problems which attracts,
and not the poetry itself. This, of course, is a great deal better
than nothing, and the poet has no right to be snooty about it: it
is quite possible that the surface meaning of his verse may be a
decoy which will lead on the un-'literary' type of reader to an
appreciation of the intrinsic poetical meaning. The self-respect-
ing poet would much prefer as an audience the 'tough' person to
the person whose education has rendered him incapable of any
activity but reading. But until this 'tough' public has got past
that meaning of poetry which can be expressed just as well in
prose, and reached the meaning which cannot be expressed except in poetry, we must not claim a poetic revival. As it is, there
are few signs even of the first stage of such a revival in interest:
poetry has not begun to be quoted in parliament again, or in the
pulpit; its obvious possibilities for snob-appeal have almost entirely evaded the evil eye of the publicist: it is still suspect in our
schools, unless written in a foreign language or capable of breed-
ing pages of 'notes': as a subject of conversation it is confined
largely to literary societies and to the refugees from modern
civilization. It would not be irrelevant, perhaps, at this stage to
enquire more closely into the causes of the neglect, not only of
modern poetry, but of all poetry —

> Whoever you are, it concerns you all
> And human glory.

CHAPTER VI

POETRY was born from magic: it grew up with religion: it lived through the age of reason: is it to die in the century of propaganda? Not death, perhaps, but a self-defensive cataleptic trance. For what hope has it of making itself heard in such a pandemonium of slogans, national anthems, headlines, tips from the horse's mouth, straight talks, loud speakers, manifestos, monkey business, madhouse gossip and high-explosive ideals? Poetry is based on the principle of free individual interpretation; you must create the meaning of each poem out of your private experience. But life for the average child of the twentieth century becomes an endless series of extension-lectures on everything under the sun; every item of his experience is explained to him—and worse, he is told exactly what his reaction to it should be. Who is he, then, to claim an individual interpretation of anything, let alone poetry? Bread, that once contained a deity, is an affair of calories now: you could put your own interpretation on the deity, but you cannot make calories mean anything but calories—they can neither receive life from your private experience nor add life to it.

... And in cold Europe, in the middle of Autumn destruction,
Christopher stood, his face grown lined with wincing
In front of ignorance—'Tell the English,' he shivered,
　'Man is a spirit' . . . .

(W. H. Auden.)

But it is too late. We know better. Man is an anatomy. The X-ray has defeated the intuition of kinship and the inspiration of solitude. There has never been complete freedom of interpretation for anyone at any time: the more vital a religion has been, the more plainly it has told man what he must believe in one direction—and the more freedom of choice and interpretation it has given him in all other directions. There is a lost world between 'This is the Catholick Faith: which except a man believe faithfully, he cannot be saved,' and 'Drink Guinness: it is good for you.' Poetry has its roots in incantation; its effect has always been to create a state of mind: but it may well despair of competing with the incantation of Big Business, Bigger Navies, Brighter Churches, and all the other gang-yells of Hell's Angels. Poetry was born from magic, and science is the great enemy of magic: for magic is the personal interpretation of the universe; science, the impersonal rationalisation. So it would seem that in a 'scientific' age the flower of poetry must wither. Yet it need not be so. As a magician can prevail against a rival witch-doctor by getting possession of some hair from his head or a few of his toe-nails, vehicles by which the rival influence may pass into the control of his own spirit, so it is possible for poetry to steal the thunder of science, to absorb these trivial business incantations and turn them to its own uses. We shall see later, I think, that poetry is beginning to learn how to do this.

That is one thing. And then another. The learning to read poetry takes as much patience and concentration as the learning to write it, and both are still more difficult outside a tradition. When the Puritans disestablished the arts from their religious foundation, the aristocratic tradition stepped in and took full charge of them. There are obvious defects in the system of patronage; but at least it kept alive the prestige of the arts, gave individual artists a definite, homogeneous audience, thus simplifying for them the problem of communication, and provided a fixed centre from which their work could radiate over society. That to read poetry is a gentlemanly occupation is not a very high class motive for reading it, but it ensured poetry against neglect; and the fact that it was snob appeal which started you reading poetry by no means prevents you from coming to comprehend its real poetic appeal. It is not much use now telling people they are not gentlemen if they don't read poetry. But a skilful publicist could easily convince, for instance, the credulous community of 'business' that a knowledge of poetry is essential for success in commerce, and the business man who began to read for the sake of the efficiency might well go on reading for the sake of the poetry. At any rate, with the decay of the aristocratic tradition, that preserved the arts as well as the pheasants of the country, came the decline of poetry as one of the more desirable luxuries.

Again, the fact of universal elementary education is inimical to poetry. It has tended to depress the culture of the minority below the point at which a full understanding of poetry becomes possible, without raising the culture of the majority to that point. Here I particularly wish to avoid being misunderstood. I am not claiming poetry as a preserve for the intellectual: that it has undoubtedly become so seems to me a thoroughly unfortunate state of affairs. A great deal of poetry is accessible to the simple, uneducated person: its dramatic quality, its music, much of its metaphor sprang from his kind of simplicity: the innocent heart, the single eye will always recognize them again. Complete unsophistication and complete sophistication—natural and acquired wisdom—are poetry's friends. It is superficial culture, the iron frost of partial self-consciousness, the treacherous thin ice of elementary knowledge, that render the approaches to poetry impassable for so many. We must be careful not to confuse susceptibility to poetry with taste in poetry. I. A. Richards, the pioneer of the Cambridge laboratory school of literature, has devoted a great deal of effort to proving by experiment that there is no such thing as natural taste in poetry. One might have made him a present of this conclusion: there are some hypotheses so obviously true that it seems scarcely worth while proving them. Tradition forms a basis for the acquiring of literary taste: it is to the acquisition of this kind of taste I referred when I said, 'the learning to read poetry takes as much patience and concentration as the learning to write it.' The uneducated man's susceptibility to the poetical, which is quite a different thing from 'taste,' may also provide a basis for it. All one can say is that, on the one hand, lack of sophistication sets up a superficial barrier to the acquisition of taste; on the other, sophistication may set up a superficial barrier to poetic susceptibility. There is nothing to show that these barriers are more than superficial.

A very much denser obstruction is in the process of being erected now by literary critics. As Stephen Spender has recently remarked: 'This is the kind of criticism which goes far to explain why so many people detest poetry. It speaks of poets as though they were superior beings incapable of experiencing the feelings of ordinary people; it translates simple and direct poetry, which easily explains itself, into high-flown and indirect language. In trying to elevate poetry, it puts it on the shelf.' In so far as this is true, it is because these critics are not really interested in poetry, but only in their own feelings. There can be only two valuable kinds of criticism. The first aims simply to erect signposts for the reader, to help him over difficult places, and to make him feel that the journey is worth undertaking. The second, creative criticism, is rare as any other form of creative writing. Where the critic has studied an author, lived with him in the spirit over a long space of time, become saturated with him, an affinity may grow up between them, so that some of the original power of the master is transmitted to the disciple. Like a great virtuoso, like Schnabel with Beethoven, the critic through his deep understanding may magnify the glory of his master: interpretation becomes an act of creation. Criticism to-day appears to be as ashamed of the first function as it is incapable of the second.

We may attribute this critical ineptitude largely to the obsolescence of the essay. While a number of admirable writers have used the essay as an art form, it must be conceded that for a far greater number of far less admirable writers it has been simply an opportunity for giving their own egos an airing. As the popularity of the essay waned, these latter deserted it and descended in a swarm upon the critical columns of our periodicals. Thus it is that we find, instead of criticism, long narcissist ramblings, the 'reviewer's' views on everything under the sun except the book that is supposed to be in question, spontaneous tributes to his own personality, literary chat, a style as mechanically exhibitionist as a shop-walker's gestures — the author's work continually used as a kind of foil, quintain, stalking-horse or what you will for the critic's ego.

The series of shrines, dedicated to themselves, which critics construct in the place of criticism, interpose a formidable barrier between poetry and the reader. A barrier of a different description was begun long ago by Puritanism. Puritanism, driven underground at the Restoration, emerged later as the 'Nonconformist Conscience': during its sojourn below ground it lost its religious fervour and single-mindedness, while its inferiority motives grew more and more pronounced. The Nonconformist Conscience infected people with a creeping conviction that there is something naughty about the arts: its inveterate feud against everything that people mean by the word 'beauty' led it to condemn poetry equally with sex as something at best flippant and at worst immoral. We see in this attitude that jealous hatred of individuality and individual achievement which is, paradoxically enough, so often combined with protestantism in religion and the dogma of free competition in trade. As commercial ethics began to break down the rather half-hearted defence put up by ecclesiastical ethics, the stress came to be laid increasingly upon the flippant rather than the immoral nature of the arts. The inferiority feeling of the Protestants when brought face to face with art now rationalized itself into a contempt of art as something unpractical and useless. This position gained strength in the eyes of the non-combatant from the indiscreet talk about Art for Art's sake that was indulged in by the nineties. It was indiscreet because it expressed a truth in a misleading, tendencious and rather defiant way: it gave the man in the street the impression that art was something quite unconnected with life as he understood the word; that its exponents claimed for themselves a superiority and wrapped themselves in a kind of noli-me-tangere professional mysticism. Unfortunately, though the practitioners of poetry have for the most part ceased maintain-

d

ing this provocative attitude, the critics — as we have seen — continue to maintain it.

At this point the reader may with some justification interject: 'But that is simply not true. It is just because the practitioners of poetry are surrounding their ideas with an atmosphere of mystery and writing above our heads that modern poetry is so repugnant to us.' And he may recall Wordsworth's strong comment on 'Poets, who think that they are conferring honour upon themselves and their art, in proportion as they separate themselves from the sympathies of men, and indulge in arbitrary and capricious habits of expression, in order to furnish food for fickle tastes, and fickle appetites, of their own creation.' Thus we are brought back to the charge of 'obscurity.' On this subject two preliminary remarks must be made. First, much post-war verse is undoubtedly obscure. Second, while some writers are of the sort to be content with a transient notoriety attained by deliberate and specious obscurification, it would not be sensible to suppose that there are none influenced by the poet's ancient longing to communicate: the reader must trust these poets for a little longer. The questions then remain, must the true poet be obscure to-day? And, if so, why?

Let us now turn back to Wordsworth's preface. 'The human mind is capable of being excited without the application of gross and violent stimulants. . . . It has therefore appeared to me, that to endeavour to produce or enlarge this capability is one of the best services in which, at any period, a writer can be engaged; but this service, excellent at all times, is especially so at the present day. For a multitude of causes, unknown to former times, are now acting with a combined force to blunt the discriminating powers of the mind, and, unfitting it for all voluntary exertion, to reduce it to a state of almost savage torpor. The most effective of these causes are the great national events which are daily taking place, and the increasing accumulation of men in cities. . . .' These words, true for his day, are true in a far more widely extended sense for our own. With the effect of 'great national events' on post-war poetry I shall deal later. The effect

of town civilization is more immediately pressing, and it con-
cerns poets in two ways.

First, there are a number of 'gross and violent stimulants,' in
the social sense, which are acting upon the mind to 'reduce it to
a state of almost savage torpor.' We have already noticed some:
advertisement and cheap publicity of every description, education having a wide extent but little depth, shots of scientific
dope. To these we must add the newspaper, the wireless, the
mass-produced novel, the cinema, all the machinery which
enables men's minds or bodies to be carried faster and farther
than their proper power of imagination or endurance could
carry them. The narcotic and unnerving property of these stimulants has been thoroughly established by far better qualified
writers than myself. For the poet their particular dangers are
either that he may be tempted to compete — to write a kind of
exciting, irritant poetry calculated to work upon the nerves in a
similar way: or that, on the other hand, disgusted with the
effects of these social agents, he may condemn the causes whole-
sale and withdraw into a world of his own where the voices of
the mechanical tempters cannot be heard. Both these dangers
contribute to poetry's present obscurity, but only, I think, in
a minor degree. It is necessary, at least, that the poet should be
aware of them, but should not run away. For, though some of
the results of modern inventions are evil, the causes must be
neither evil nor good: they cover wide tracts of life to-day, and
it is neither desirable to run away from life, nor possible to run
away from it except into a state of living death.

It is of prime importance for poets to be warned that all these
products of town civilization are damnable only in so far as they
imply the outrunning of man's psychological development by
the complexities of his environment, the destruction of the
creator by the elaboration of his own creations.

> . . . Remember the ringed ammonite, running
> Crazy was killed for being too clever. . . .

When his mind fails to stay the pace set by its inventions,

madness must ensue. Which brings us to the second main effect of town civilization upon poetry and to the root cause of its present obscurity. In a word, this is the expansion of the social unit to a size at which it becomes impossible for the individual to have any real contact with his fellows and thus to benefit from the group. Towns, founded by men's desire to live together, now compel them to live separately. The individual has a certain definite range and radius of sympathy, comprehension, imagination: this radius, for the average man, has slowly enlarged with the progress of civilization: civilization is, in fact, finally to be measured by the diameter of the circle of the 'average' man's imagination. All went comparatively well till the beginning of the nineteenth century, when a spate of inventions swelled the social unit so rapidly that it burst and disintegrated. Now the successful social unit is one which both adapts itself to the slowly widening circumferences of individual imaginations and is in itself the cause of their extension. The social and the individual unit obviously are interactive, so that with the sudden nightmare swelling of the former we got a similar morbid growth of the latter. Thus the gravest charge to be laid against the cinema, the radio, the newspaper and the various easy modes of transit is that they are all enlarging the field of individual experience so rapidly that communication between centre (soul) and circumference (imagination) is in danger of being snapped. The individual is being pulled out so forcibly in all directions that his personal life is attenuated and dissipated.

Now a compact, working social group has the same advantage for a poet as tradition: it enables him to take a number of things for granted. He is aware instinctively of the average radius of individual experience and imagination, and he can use this knowledge in that task which Wordsworth pronounced to be one of the best services in which a writer can be engaged, the task of producing or enlarging the capability of men's minds for being excited. It is noticeable that the greatest achievements of poetry and the most prolific periods of poetry have arisen in small, compact, homogeneous communities such as the Greek city state or Elizabethan England. Where the community is swollen, spiritually disorganized and heterogeneous; where there is no widely accepted system of morals and no clearly defined circumference of imagination—(I have used imagination throughout in the psychological sense); the poet's data are terribly confused and his task correspondingly difficult. In the face of this intolerable complexity, the sensitive individual feels compelled to retire upon himself, to create artificially for himself a world of manageable proportions: this is not necessarily psychological introversion, but may be a salutary act of antagonism to an environment whose complications are choking his life. This act—a kind of starting again at the beginning—is being performed in post-war poetry. 'Even in the midst of the tornadoed Atlantic of my being do I myself still centrally disport in mute calm.' The poet now is seeking to find and establish that central calm, a point from which he may begin to work outward again; and in the process he is bound to be obscure, for he is talking to himself and to his friends—to that tiny, temporarily isolated unit with which communication is possible, with whom he can take a certain number of things for granted.

This in itself is the first clue; when properly grasped, it will lead us a long way towards the understanding of recent poetry. For in this poetry there is a perpetual interplay of private and public meaning: the inner circle of communication—the poet's conversation with his own arbitrarily isolated social group—is perpetually widening into and becoming identified with the outer circles of his environment; and conversely, the specifically modern data of his environment—the political situation, the psychological states, the scientific creations of twentieth-century man—are again and again used to reflect the inner activities of the poet. Such interchange of personal and (in the widest sense) political imagery, such interaction of personal and political feeling is to be found in poem after poem of the younger writers. It is my own experience that, when I have expressed some private experience in a poem, I have frequently discovered it to contain a 'political' significance of which I was quite unconscious while writing it. A year or two ago I wrote a sequence called 'From Feathers to Iron' which for me expressed simply my thoughts and feelings during the nine months before the birth of my first child: the critics, almost to a man, took it for a political allegory; the simple, personal meaning evaded them.

The poet to-day, I have said, is as it were starting again at the beginning. His starting point, therefore, is love. We shall not begin to understand post-war poetry until we realize that the poet is appealing above all for the creation of a society in which the real and living contact between man and man may again become possible. That is why, speaking from the living unit of himself and his friends, he appeals for the contraction of the social group to a size at which human contact may again be established and demands the destruction of all impediments to love. Listen:

> Comrades to whom our thoughts return,
> Brothers for whom our bowels yearn
>   When words are over;
> Remember that in each direction
> Love outside our own election
> Holds us in unseen connection:
>   O trust that ever.

(W. H. Auden.)

> You who go out alone, on tandem, or on pillion,
> Down arterial roads riding in April,
> Or sad beside lakes where hill-slopes are reflected
> Making fires of leaves, your high hopes fallen:
> Cyclists and hikers in company, day excursionists,
> Refugees from cursed towns and devastated areas;
> Know you seek a new world, a saviour to establish
> Long-lost kinship and restore the blood's fulfilment.

(C. Day Lewis.)

Readers of this strange language,
We have come at last to a country
Where light equal, like the shine from snow, strikes all faces,
Here you may wonder
How it was that works, money, interest, building, could ever
    hide
The palpable and obvious love of man for man.

(Stephen Spender.)

CHAPTER VII

IT might seem inevitable that, in a world so inimical apparently both to poetry and to the social ideals which living poets affirm, the main poetic instrument would be satire. Yet little poetic satire is being written, and the best of it—that of Auden—is scarcely recognisable as such by those accustomed to thinking of satire in terms of Juvenal, Dryden or Pope. Satirical verse has always been directed either against personal enemies or against social abuses. Of the former variety there is not much to be found to-day: Roy Campbell's 'Georgiad,' occasional poems by Osbert Sitwell and Humbert Wolfe spring to mind; such work too often affects one as being little more than pastiche of eighteenth-century satire. One feels that the style has generated the hate. It is, indeed, a little shabby, a little insignificant: not really hate at all, but spite; and it takes a very remarkable poet, like Pope, and one thoroughly assured of his own position, to elevate malice into hate. It is as true for personal as for social satire that the poet must learn to love before he can begin to hate. Besides, the throwing open of so large an acreage of review columns to anyone who cares to become an occupier has given writers a wider field for the conducting in public of private vendettas than could now be afforded by satirical verse.

Anyone acquainted with the literature of the first decade after the war must have noticed a prevailing tone of disgust and a kind of wry-smiling self-contempt. That was our substitute for satire. Murder, greed, lechery, cruelty, cant, all the tricks of the spiritual poisoner—the satirist can deal with these separately and in manageable proportions: but in the face of so versatile and universal an agent of wickedness as the Great War, in the face of a whole world gone crazy, the satirist's breath was taken away. Knowing himself infected by the general madness, he realized that his first business was to heal himself. He began to laugh, not at the crimes and follies of others, but at his own

debility and insignificance. This self-flagellation was a morbid
yet a salutary process. We see it anticipated in the well-known
lines of Eliot from 'Prufrock':

> No! I am not Prince Hamlet, nor was meant to be;
> Am an attendant lord, one that will do
> To swell a progress, start a scene or two,
> Advise the prince; no doubt, an easy tool,
> Deferential, glad to be of use,
> Politic, cautious, and meticulous:
> Full of high sentence, but a bit obtuse;
> At times, indeed, almost ridiculous —
> Almost, at times, the Fool.

When the satirist had got the poison out of his own system,
he found himself still at a loss. For social satire must be founded
on the firm basis of an established society and a generally accepted moral code: it is, in practice, inclined to be reactionary;
to attack aberration from an order that may be decaying but is
certainly the status quo. I have said 'the poet must learn to love
before he can begin to hate:' the satirist founds his hate of the
present on his love of the past, his hatred of particular flaws in
society on his love of the whole architecture of that society.
Where that structure is not so much decadent as shot to pieces,
where an iron curtain seems to have shut down between him and
the past, the poet has no basis for satire left. There is plenty to
attack, but no favourable ground from which the attack may be
launched.

At this point three men of great powers set out to find a basis.
Wyndham Lewis retired to the heights of Reason, D. H. Lawrence dug himself in in the Unconscious, and T. S. Eliot took
over the position of Anglo-Catholicism. It is, perhaps, a sufficient comment on this last position that a man of such poetic
ability as Eliot should have found himself incapable of launching
a satiric attack from it. Wyndham Lewis, though he stands head
and shoulders above almost every other contemporary writer in
England, has impaired his value as a satirist through allowing

himself to be ostentatiously embittered by the indifference and
hostility with which his earlier work was received. The spec-
tacle of a man of such powers making capital out of the representation of himself as the giant baited by pigmies, is a little
melancholy and disgusting. This theatrical attitude pervades his
lately published verse satire, 'One Way Song.' But Lewis's
prose analyses of our present failings have given poets a number
of lines on which to work and set them an example of intellectual
honesty. In his exposure of the flight from reason and all its consequences, particularly the infantility-cults and the arrested mental development of the modern European, we may find the clue
to many apparently obscure utterances of post-war poets. Apart
from anything else, he has done enormous service in helping to
create a new tradition for them: he enables them to take a number of things for granted.

Yet, although Lewis's analysis convinces us again and again
as being correct in detail, we are compelled to feel that Lawrence rather than Lewis had got hold of the right end of the
stick. Lewis's knowledge is the knowledge of the statistician,
Lawrence's that of the poet. In so far as he was a prophet he
went, like any other prophet, to extremes. But, when we have
cut away all his errors, exaggerations, prejudices and nonsense,
we shall find a hard core of truth more valuable possibly than
the whole sum of Lewis's work. This truth is, simply, that the
cerebral part of civilized man has been forced into unnatural
growth at the expense of the soil, the rest of him; that the conscious has outstripped the unconscious and this cutting of communication has rendered impossible a healthy give-and-take
between the two. As he himself said in 'Pansies':

> Man is immoral because he has got a mind
> And can't get used to the fact.

Once he arrives at the home truths that lie behind the exasperation and frequent vagueness of 'Pansies' and the mystical hyper-
bole of the 'Fantasia of the Unconscious,' the reader will find

much that is difficult in post-war poetry becoming plain. He
will also, incidentally, be made aware of a tendency towards a
new kind of sentimentality growing up within it. Lawrence
cannot be held responsible for this. He knew pretty exactly
what he meant by such often used symbols as 'the blood' and
'the sun.' But several of us younger poets have been guilty of
using them in a false romantic way, so as to give a borrowed
radiance to a poem and not so as to reflect its own nature. We
may suspect such mal-digested influence in lines like: —

> . . . Because now
> like the sun on my loins
> unafraid and possessive
> I have life: . . .
>
> (John Pudney.)

It is possible that 'Pansies' was the forerunner of a new genus
of satire. If this proves true, then the date of Freud's 'Introduc-
tory Lectures' will be recognized as one of the important dates
for English poetry. Lawrence's appeal for fair play for the unconscious derived from the psycho-analysts. At a time when the
traditional moral standards were being questioned or discarded,
Freud and his followers began to suggest quite seriously what
Samuel Butler had said half in fun, that virtue was health and
vice a sickness. We are not now concerned with the finality or
extent of truth in this judgment. The point is that it gained a
widespread credence among the cultured class in Europe and so
gave poets some sort of basis, if only a temporary one, for the
'criticism of life.' It completely took the edge off the old weapons
of satire: the satirist had used sword and dagger; now he must
take up the scalpel.

> Some dream, say yes, long coiled in the ammonite's slumber
> Is uncurling, prepared to lay on our talk and kindness,
> Its military silence, its surgeon's idea of pain.
>
> (W. H. Auden.)

Auden himself is the pre-eminent satirist in this mode. His first book, *Poems*, is full of psychological examples and inferences. It ought, by rights, to have been nothing more than an illustrated case-book. Yet no one can read it without feeling again and again, however baffled he may be for a meaning, the impact of poetry. It is his astonishing capacity for assimilation and his ability to distil poetry out of the most forbidding retorts of science, which make me think that Auden more than any other young writer has the essential qualifications of a major poet. The subject-matter of his verse would seem to be irretrievably 'prosaic'; yet, if we try to express almost any poem of his in prose, we find it impossible; its rare spirit evaporates in the process. The attitude of the satirist is for him halfway between the attitudes of the psycho-therapist and the faith-healer: sometimes he is carried to ridiculous lengths by the latter, infuriating the reader with an apparently superstitious belief in the functional nature of all disease. But even when he is being most ridiculous, his work keeps its poetic interest intact. When he is sensible and sober, the result is very good indeed.

> Sir, no man's enemy, forgiving all
> But will his negative inversion, be prodigal:
> Send to us power and light, a sovereign touch
> Curing the intolerable neural itch,
> The exhaustion of weaning, the liar's quinsy,
> And the distortions of ingrown virginity.
> Prohibit sharply the rehearsed response
> And gradually correct the coward's stance;
> Cover in time with beams those in retreat
> That, spotted, they turn though the reverse were great;
> Publish each healer that in city lives
> Or country houses at the end of drives;
> Harrow the house of the dead: look shining at
> New styles of architecture, a change of heart.

Gerard Manley Hopkins addressed God as 'Sir.' Negativism, the deathwill, will's inversion — Lawrence spent half his life dinning that into our ears. Lines 4-10 are material that may be found in any psychiatric text-book. Yet the result is a poem, and one that could have been written by no one but Auden. The satirist of this type is theoretically no man's enemy, in the sense that he can call nothing evil but 'will his negative inversion.' For him the suicide is a point at which the infected matter of a diseased society is discharged; the murderer, too, is a safety-valve, a scape-goat—'The murderer shall be wreathed with flowers; he shall die for the people.' In practice, however, Auden gives the effect of being as intolerant and aggressive as any of the traditional satirists, for he seems able to find an inexhaustible supply of victims of will's negative inversion. When we read 'The Orators' we find, gathered together in the person of 'the Enemy,' an enormous variety of symptoms of this psychological deadly sin: in him Auden attacks the death-will, the morbid self-consciousness that cancels human contacts and defeats action, the man for ever on the defensive against life, the coward. No extract can do justice to the scope and fertility of imagination, the extraordinary mixture of sense and superstition, of schoolboyish exuberance and adult intuition, which are to be found in this book. But here is a glimpse of his healer:

> See him take off his coat and get down with a spanner
> To each unhappy Joseph and repressed Diana,
> Say Bo to the invalids and take away their rugs,
> The war-memorials decorate with member-mugs.
> The gauche and the lonely he will introduce of course
> To the smaller group, the right field of force;
> The few shall be taught who want to understand,
> Most of the rest shall love upon the land;
> Living in one place with a satisfied face
> All of the women and most of the men
> Shall work with their hands and not think again. . . .

'What do you think about England, this country of ours where nobody is well?' Auden asks at the beginning of 'The Orators': and by consistently maintaining this attitude he has done more perhaps than any other writer to replace in our minds the idea of the wickedness of society by the idea of the sickness of society.

The force of his satire is, however, diminished in two ways. First, he does not seem to discriminate sufficiently between the really sick and the merely hypochondriac: the old satirists had to have a very definite criterion for measuring good and evil; the new one, to be thoroughly successful, must have equally definite standards of sickness and health. Auden is an adept at saying Bo to invalids and taking away their rugs; but one feels that he does not really care whether the invalid is a malingerer or just recovering from pneumonia. He is an expert at diagnosis, but has only one treatment for all ailments: we should feel happier if he evinced a love of health and a knowledge of its nature equivalent to his love and ability of diagnosis. In the second place his treatment, his method of satire is apt to defeat its own ends. Spender has correctly called it 'buffoon-poetry'; and in guying his victims Auden too often becomes identified with them, so that, instead of the relationship between satirist and victim which alone can give significance to satire we get a series of figures of fun into each of whom the satirist temporarily disappears. Where light and darkness merge into one, the visibility is poor and our eyes will play us tricks. If Auden could maintain an objective attitude to his victims, if the part of him that writes buffoon-poetry could be brought into closer relationship with his positive poetic force and be modified by it—or, in other words, if he had a coherent philosophy at his back, nothing could stop him from writing major poetry. At present he suffers from an extreme sensitiveness to the impact of ideas combined with an incapacity to relate them with any scheme of values, which is apt to give his work a flavour of intellectual dilettantism. But in the meantime, we can be quite content with the power that enables his satirical self to be as funny as:

> Lord Baden-Powell with a piece of string
> Was proving that reef-knots honour the King. . . .

or, of the unhappy poet who fled—

> To islands in your private seas
> Where thoughts like castaways find ease
>   In endless petting.

CHAPTER VIII

IT is a truism that a sound society makes for sound individuals, and sound individuals instance a sound society. For the post-war poet, living in a society undeniably sick, that truism has turned into a dilemma. We have seen him on the one hand rendered more acutely conscious of individuality by the acceptance of current psychological doctrines; and on the other hand, rendered both by poetic intuition and ordinary observation acutely conscious of the present isolation of the individual and the necessity for a social organism which may restore communion. He looks to one side and he sees D. H. Lawrence, the extreme point of individualism in this century's literature, its zenith or its nadir: he admits the force of Lawrence's appeal, but he has watched him driven from continent to continent, driven ill and mad, a failure unable to recreate a satisfactory social group from the nucleus of his own individuality. He looks to the other side and he sees Communism, proclaiming—though with a different meaning from Lawrence's—'revolution for life's sake,' the most whole-hearted attempt ever made to raise the individual to his highest power by a conditioning of his environment: yet here too he notices the bully and the spy, and wonders if any system can expel and survive that poison.

So there arises in him a conflict; between the old which his heart approves and the new which fructifies his imagination; between the idea of a change of heart that should change society and the idea of a new society making a new man; between individual education and mass economic conditionment. At which end should one begin? The poet, you will say, has no business to be trespassing: if he will wander into other people's fields, he must take the consequences. But it is not as simple as that. The poet, besides being a poet, is also a man, 'fed with the same food, hurt with the same weapons' as other men. Where there is hope in the air, he will hear it; where there is agony about, he will feel it. He must feel as a man what he reveals as a poet. It is as absurd to tell him that he must only feel strongly about

natural scenery as it is to call every 'nature-poet' an escapist.
Nor is it right for us to say that the poet should be concerned
only with eternal facts, with summer and winter, birth, marriage and death. These are the mountain-peaks, the final and
everlasting limits of his known world, but they are always the
background against which stand out and are measured temporal
things—the rise and fall of cities, the year's harvest, the moment's pain. To-day the foreground is a number of fluid, confused and contradictory patterns. Standing at the end of an
epoch, the poet's arms are stretched out to opposite poles, the
old life and the new; that is his power and his crucifixion.

> Come down, come down, you suffering man,
> Come down, and high or low
> Follow your fancy and go with us
> The way that we should go.
>
> That cannot be till two agree
> Who long have lain apart:
> Traveller, know, I am here to show
> Your own divided heart.   (C. Day Lewis.)

Standing as a man between two worlds, he stands as a poet
between two fires. On the one hand the Communist tells him
that he is no better than a dope-peddler unless he 'joins the revolution,' that he is unhappy and ineffective because he is trying
to live in two worlds at once, and that (although the achievements of 'bourgeois' art are undeniable and to be respected) the
function of artists at the present crisis is to help lead men out of
the bourgeois position towards the proletarian, to be propa-
gandists for the new world. On the other hand, the bourgeois
critic rebukes him for allowing a sympathy with Communism
to drive him into a kind of writing that at any rate sounds very
like propaganda, asserting that an ideology is only useful to the
poet in so far as it is felt and that ideas, whether revolutionary or
reactionary, must never be more to the poet than the raw
material out of which his poetry is formed.

They are both right up to a point. Yet the bourgeois critic must remember that there is no reason why poetry should not also be propaganda; the effect of invocation, of poetry, and of propaganda is to create a state of mind; and it is not enough to say that poetry must do unconsciously what propaganda does consciously, for that would be to dismiss all didactic poetry from that of the Bible downwards. All one can say is that propaganda verse is to be condemned when the didactic is achieved at the expense of the poetic: poetry, in fact, whatever else it may or may not be, must be poetry—a sound, if obvious, conclusion. In this context we may instance the reception of Auden's recent work 'The Dance of Death.' It is compared unfavourably with his earlier books largely on the ground that it is propaganda: but the 'Poems' and 'The Orators' were full of propaganda too; they told the Englishman, particularly the middle-class Englishman, in a variety of subtle ways, that he is half-dead. And if a powerful writer insists for long enough that you are half-dead, why, then, you begin to realize or believe it; the insistent suggestion puts you in that frame of mind: poetry has been propaganda. So 'The Dance of Death,' if it is to be criticized, must be criticized as poetry and not for being propaganda.

'Poems' and 'The Orators' are didactic from an individualist psychological standpoint. 'The Dance of Death' is an attempt at didactic writing from a Marxian standpoint. If it fails, the failure must be imputed to the fact that the classless society is not established in England, for we have seen that social satire requires an established system from which to work: the poet cannot satirize the present in the uncertain light of the future. Should Communism come to be the settled system in England, we might then expect a great renaissance of satire. And that must be our first answer to the Communist critic. The poet is a sensitive instrument, not a leader. Ideas are not material for the poetic mind until they have become commonplaces for the 'practical' mind. On the other hand, when the Communist tells the poet that he must 'join the revolution,' he is right in the sense that there can

e

be no divorce for the Marxist between theory and practice, and that only revolutionary activity can make a revolutionary poet. Nothing, however, is to be gained by accusing the poet of employing each poem as a solution of his own difficulties, of drugging himself and thus unfitting himself through his poetry to be a happy class-warrior. The poet is made like that, he has to protest; and while it is true, in a sense, that each poem solves its own conflict, it is only a temporary solution; his agonies of mind are drugged, perhaps, but not ended. Again, too much has been made of the adverse effect of so-called 'revolutionary' poetry upon a potentially revolutionary public. Spender has written: 'The people who had read these poems would linger over certain aspects of materialism, they would forget, in the course of their meditations, the social revolution. . . . From the point of view of the revolutionary propagandist art plays amongst the more intelligent and less satisfied members of the leisured classes the same rôle as charity plays amongst the poor. Where there should be friction leading to a final break-down it oils the machine and enables it to go on running.' That is the conventional Communist attitude, too: but it is by no means all the truth. The drug-fiend will get drugs somewhere: if he finds his poppy and mandragora in poetry, you must blame his habit, not the poet. But a poetry sympathetic to Communism can strike home to sounder hearts than these: it can awaken interest, kindle indignation that may spread wildfire, not flicker out in private; it can cause conversions and hasten a decline. The revolutionary poet is not a leader: he stands, like a mirror at the crossroads, showing the traffic, the danger, the way you have come and the ways you may go—'your own divided heart.' He must give courage by reflecting your own courage, and forward revolution by reflecting your own will to it.

Communism did not begin to affect British poetry till some fifteen years after the October revolution. In 1931 'Hugh McDiarmid' published his 'First Hymn to Lenin.' Most of his poetry is written in the Scots vernacular, which may account for the neglect in England of such admirable stuff as his earlier 'A drunk man looks at the Thistle,' and 'Circumjack Cencrastus.' In these works the influence of Eliot is apparent; but there is also a bluntness, a harshness, and a mixture of metaphysical ecstasy and mundane uncouth wildness, which are peculiarly national. The 'First Hymn to Lenin' shows the drunk man sober, the high-flying metaphysician descended to a solid, materialist earth. The title poem of this book begins:

> Few even o' the criminals, cravens, and fools
> Wha's voices vilify a man they ken
> They've cause to fear and are unfit to judge
> As they're to stem his influence again
> But in the hollows where their herts should be
>   Foresee your victory.
> Churchills, Locker-Lampsons, Beaverbrooks'll be
> In history's perspective less to you
> (And them!) than the centurions to Christ
> Of whom, as you, at least this muckle's true
> 'Tho' pairtly wrang he cam' to richt amang's
>   Faur greater wrangs.'...

Two things may be pointed out here. First, the suggestion—to be taken up and made into a kind of technique of hetero-suggestion by Auden, that the upholders of our present system are beginning to feel defeat in their bones. Second, a reasonableness, a refusal to be stampeded into fanaticism, which is noticeable in even such definitely revolutionary English writers as R.E. Warner; a quality which, though it may be dismissed by some as compromise, will appeal to others as common sense. In 'The Seamless Garment,' one of McDiarmid's best poems, we find this quality at work, producing a calm and reasoned certainty that is most impressive. The poet is speaking to a cousin in a cloth-mill, comparing Lenin's work with the work of Rilke in a different sphere and both with a weaver's; and first, of Lenin—

> ... His secret and the secret o' a'
> That's worth ocht.
> The shuttles fleein' owre quick for my een
> Prompt the thocht,
> And the co-ordination atween
> Weaver and machine.
>
> The haill shop's dumfounderin'
> To a stranger like me.
> Second nature to you; you're perfectly able
> To think, speak and see
> Apairt frae the looms, tho' to some
> That doesna sae easily come.
>
> Lenin was like that wi' workin' class life.
> At hame wi't a'.
> His fause movements couldna' been fewer,
> The best weaver Earth ever saw.
> A' he'd to dae wi' moved intact
> Clean, clear, and exact. ...

He goes on presently to express that feeling which is at the back of a great deal of the poetry written in the last few years, the feeling that the system under which we live deprives the majority of the chance of a decent life.

> ... Are you equal to life as to the loom?
> Turnin' oot shoddy or what?
> Claith better than man? D'ye live to the full,
> Your poo'er's a' deliverly taught?
> Or scamp a' thing else? Border cloth's famous.
> Shall things o' mair consequence shame us? ...
>
> ... The womenfolk ken what I mean.
> Things maun fit like a glove,
> Come clean off the spoon — and syne
> There's time for life and love.
> The mair we mak' natural as breathin the mair
> Energy for ither things we'll can spare
> But as lang as we bide like this
> Neist to naething we ha'e, or miss. ...

The 'First Hymn to Lenin' was followed by a rush of poetry sympathetic to Communism or influenced by it. 'New Signatures' (1932) showed the beginning of this trend; 'New Country' (1933) contained definitely Communist forms by Auden, Charles Madge, R. E. Warner and others: Spender's 'Poems' and my own 'Magnetic Mountain,' both published in 1933, continued the movement. But here a word of warning should be interposed. In estimating the social importance of this movement, we must be careful to discount the temporary and fictitious impetus it received from the economic slump of this period, and to remember that the literary world is no less prone to fashion than any other. Its desire at this point for a wider contact with the world as a whole coincided with the coming into fashion of Soviet Russia as a subject for intellectual discussion, and we shall be right in thinking that the connection between the two is not above suspicion. Already, as the slump shows signs in England of another feverish rise to another temporary boom, we note a slackening of Communist enthusiasm in poetry: certain of the rats are swimming back to a ship which does not seem to be sinking this time after all. But this use of Communism both as a stimulus and as a kind of relief from irritation, its distortion into a personal religion, can only be short-lived and superficial: the demands of Communism are too imperative, too clear-cut for the writer who wants only the cessation of mental pain and a private peace in his own time.

We shall probably find in the near future a cleavage in this poetical movement. Communist ideology and symbolism will be very much less obtrusive in poetry: for those who, as men, made Communism the nearest port in a storm, and as poets assumed it as the fashionable dress of the moment, will have departed elsewhere; while others, having made up their minds and taken it to heart, will be producing work of which Communism is the foundation and the integral framework, not the decoration and façade. Such poetry will, of course, not be communist, proletarian poetry: we could not expect that till a classless society existed in fact. To the orthodox criticism that the poet should never associate himself with any system, political or economic, except to the extent that its ideas provide stimulus and material for his poetry, I should answer by stressing the distinction made above between the poet as a man and the poet as a poet. It is a question not so much of æsthetic theory as of fact. A man, by developing the poetic faculty in himself, does not automatically secede from his common humanity. It is true that some artists have cultivated the former successfully to the almost complete exclusion of the latter, and some but by no means all great poets have been—in Keats's phrase—men that 'have not any individuality, any determined character.' But this kind of passive, plastic nature, where the whole man is metamorphosed into an impersonal poetic instrument, is, I believe, rare. In most poets there is an intermittent conflict between the poetic self and the rest of the man; and it is by reconciling the two, not by eliminating the one, that they can reach their full stature. I can agree with Eliot's statement that 'the more perfect the artist, the more completely separate in him will be the man who suffers and the mind which creates,' but it must be realized that 'separate' means 'distinct,' and not 'unconnected.' It is this conflict more than anything else which drives artists to drugs, dissipation, madness or death, and the conflict is bound to be particularly acute in a state of society that is inimical to the well-being of humanity as a whole and therefore both obstructs and challenges the artist's own humanity. So we may say that, while the poetic function of the man cannot be directly concerned with political ideas, his humanity may be concerned with them; in which case, they will inevitably come into communication with his poetical function and to some extent affect his poetry.

We may go further and say that, if a poet is going to bereceptive of political ideas, it is essential for him as a man to feel strongly about them. For this strong 'human' emotion, working upon ideas, makes them a more tractable material for poetry; the poetic faculty will, in fact, have to deal—not with an abstract idea, — but with an idea suffused and moulded by emotion; and that is a common subject for poetry. What is really undesirable is that the poet should have dealings with political ideas as a poet without first having feelings about them as a man: for direct contact between the poetic function and abstract ideas can give birth only to rhetoric. The man must pass the idea through the medium of his emotion before the poet can get to work upon it.

'We make out of the quarrel with others rhetoric,' Yeats has said, 'but of the quarrel with ourselves, poetry.' This conception of the quarrel with ourselves has, I believe, a twofold significance. It conveys first the idea of spiritual doubt as a poetic agent (we have seen this conflict at work in Gerard Manley Hopkins). And secondly it expresses the opposition between the divided selves of the poet, his poetic self and his 'human' self, a conflict of which Yeats has always been acutely aware. Yeats's own magnificent political poems — 'Easter 1916,' for instance, or 'Sixteen Dead Men' — are sufficient proof that a deep feeling about political ideas and events is not necessarily synonymous with that 'quarrel with others' which produces only rhetoric. Unsuccessful propaganda verse *is* an example of this kind of rhetoric: it is the result of the poet trying to convince others without having experienced either uncertainty or conviction himself; or else, of his not being a poet: the 'quarrel with others' must, for the poet, be expressed in terms of the quarrel with himself. And failure to do this accounts for the failure of much so-called revolutionary verse.

It accounts, also, to a certain extent, for its frequent vagueness. It is not asked that poetry should offer naked argument and skeleton plans. But English revolutionary verse of to-day is too often neither poetry nor effective propaganda for the cause it is intended to support. Its vague *cris-de-cœur* for a new world, its undirected and undisciplined attack upon the whole world-broad front of the status quo, are apt to produce work which makes the neutral reader wonder whether it is aimed to win him for the communist or the fascist state. Here again the influence of D. H. Lawrence assists to confuse the issue. We find, for instance, in Auden's preoccupation with the search for 'the truly strong man,' Lawrence's evangel of spiritual submission to the great individual: 'All men say they want a leader. Then let them in their souls submit to some greater soul than theirs.' And though this does not necessarily contradict communist theory, it is likely in practice to give a fascist rather than a communist tone to poetry.

There are, however, poems recently written which show that the writer has emotionally experienced a political situation and assimilated it through his specific function into the substance of poetry. It is of this kind of poetry that Wilfrid Owen is the real ancestor. It is animated by the same unsentimental pity and sacred indignation. It does not wish to make poetic capital out of the suffering of others. As Spender says in a poem about the unemployed:

> ... No, I shall weave no tracery of pen-ornament
> To make them birds upon my singing tree.

It is simple and emphatic. It gets probably as near to communist poetry as bourgeois writers under a bourgeois régime can hope to get. And it suggests the lines on which such writers must work for the present. In the following extracts we see the capitalist and the communist worlds contracted.

> Take it away,
> the sun, the light of day,
> the knitted life and start
> and pulse of heart.
> We who have not begun
> don't need the sun,
> We only have to die, to lie down
> safe in the grave from gun, from frown,
> from sick smile, from leering
> from remedy, from ghost jeering.

Now must die out
both sob and shout,
the long athletic stride,
all poise, all pride,
since men born to act
are stifled under fact
mole deep, must burrow down, not swing in sky
eagles to take the sun in eye. . . .

                              (R. E. Warner.)

Death is another milestone on their way.
With laughter on their lips and with winds blowing round them
They record simply
How this one excelled all others in making driving belts.

This is festivity, it is the time of statistics
When they record what one unit contributed:
They are glad as they lay him back in the earth
And thank him for what he gave them.

They walk home remembering the straining red flags,
And with pennons of song still fluttering through their blood
They speak of the world state
With its towns like brain-centres and its pulsing arteries. . . .

                              (Stephen Spender.)

CHAPTER IX

THE Romantic movement in England destroyed the convention of a specialized poetic diction. It is possible that Eliot and the post-war poets will be chiefly recognized by posterity as the inaugurators of a movement which finally destroyed the convention of a specialized poetic vocabulary. The field of sense-data has been very considerably enlarged in the last 150 years, and it is generally admitted now that there are no sense-data necessarily ineligible for poetic metaphor: it is no longer accepted by the poet that a factory has not the qualifications for poetic treatment possessed by a flower. It will be objected that the modern poet is not inaugurating anything here: both Shakespeare and the metaphysical school took their material, not only from the preserve of traditionally 'poetical' objects, but from the whole field of the senses and the intellect. Even Dr Johnson had to grant of the metaphysicals that 'if their conceits were farfetched, they were often worth the carriage.' But although both they and Shakespeare were successful in their treatment of conventionally alien objects, they left no permanent solution of the problems of treatment for later poets. Shakespeare's imagination was a furnace of unique intensity; his metaphors when extracted and examined apart from their context, are found to contain the most definite, concrete and often un-'poetical' words: but his imagination worked at so high a temperature that no object, however solid, angular, and tough failed to be fused into the material texture of his poetry. One cannot base a poetical theory on that heavenly fire. On the other hand, if we consider the work of Donne, Vaughan, Herbert and Crashaw, we find that their solution is not many more degrees helpful to the modern poet. Eliot well expressed it when he said that for them the intellect was at this period 'immediately at the tips of the senses': their poetry at its best gives the effect of having been composed by a kind of simultaneous operation of the senses and the intellect, as though at one and the same time they had become aware of the emotional quality of an experience and its logical implications. Whether or no their power was the result of a peculiar psychological conformation common to these writers, it was soon abandoned and the secret of it now appears to be lost. We notice occasional lines that recall it to us. Roy Campbell's poem, 'Choosing a Mast,' contains one:

> ... Who now of the white spray must take the veil ...

And there is, for another instance, Auden's —

> ... Do thoughts grow like feathers, the dead end of life.

Or Randall Swingler's —

> ... the sun-sifted birches'
> Light behaviour and the childish wind's agility.

But such lines too often lack the final concentration of the metaphysical poets, being outcrops from work of quite different texture. When the modern poet tries to rediscover their secret, he finds himself producing pastiche which is closely akin to the mere wit-writing into which they frequently degenerated without achieving their poetry.

At the same time there are affinities between the metaphysicals and the post-war poetry which go deeper than any occasional resemblances in diction. It is agreed that the influence of the French Symbolists, transmitted to a large extent through Eliot's verse, has been one of the most important formative agents of post-war verse technique. Both Eliot and Edmund Wilson have called attention to the kinship between the French Symbolists and the English metaphysicals. Wilson outlines the similarities: 'The medley of images; the deliberately mixed metaphors; the combination of passion and wit—of the grand and the prosaic manners; the bold amalgamation of material with spiritual.' And again, speaking of Corbière's poetry, he calls it 'a poetry of the outcast: often colloquial and homely, yet with a rhetoric of fantastic slang; often with the manner of slapdash doggerel, yet sure of its own morose artistic effects.' Exclude the word 'morose,' and the passage gives an exact description of Auden's work. That combination 'of the grand and the prosaic manners,' a constant alternation of the magniloquent and the colloquial, is a quality shared by Donne, Wilfrid Owen and Auden, and it is probably more from Owen than from Donne or the Symbolists that Auden derives it. The salient difference between the technique of the metaphysicals on the one hand and that of the symbolists and the English post-war poets on the other boils down to the incessant employment of witwriting by the former and its comparative neglect by the latter. The general effect obtained by each is very similar. But the metaphysicals obtained it more through the juxtaposition of superficially unrelated *Ideas* and through verbal paradox—they are working always within a logical framework, surprising and exciting us by the fantastic liberties they take within this framework: whereas the other writers in question obtain their effect more through the juxtaposition of superficially unrelated *images;* the intellectual thread is not, as in the case of the metaphysicals, knotted and ravelled, but cut; and the paradoxes are predominantly sensual rather than predominantly intellectual. It is true, as Wilson says, they both rely partly on a 'medley of images,' but the metaphysicals steeped this medley of images in an intellectual solution, while the Symbolists leave them—so to speak—to stew in their own juice.

The post-war, like the seventeenth-century, poets have inherited a world flooded with a spate of scientific theory and invention, and disturbed by many cross-currents of political and philosophic thought. I have touched on their reactions to the new trends of psychology and politics: it remains to see how they deal with the new data of science. In discussing the apparent temperamental antagonism between science and poetry, I suggested that poets to-day were learning the magician's trick of getting control over his antagonist by getting possession of his hair or his nails. Modern poets are making strenuous attempts to tap the power of science by absorbing scientific data into their work: by 'scientific data' I mean the myriad new sense-data which scientific development has put before us. The desirability of this absorption is generally recognized: the methods by which it may be achieved are by no means finally worked out, but we shall find they approximate closely to those of the metaphysicals and were sketched out by the Symbolists. At this point the reader may ask why, seeing that these new data have been accumulating since the Industrial Revolution, they were put to no use by the nineteenth-century English poets; and he may argue that what they left well alone might be left equally well alone by their successors.

I have suggested that 'ideas are not material for the poetic mind until they have become commonplaces for the "practical" mind.' I was then referring to 'ideas' in the popular sense of 'theories': but I believe this also to hold good for ideas in the philosophical meaning of 'sense-impressions.' The wit of the metaphysicals was pointed with the tough iron of science. I believe that such metal must go through a twofold process before it can be used in poetry. Scientific data must first be assimilated by the general consciousness and integrated with the whole environment; then they must undergo a further process of digestion in the individual poetic organs. It would be ridiculous to dogmatize about first and second; the two processes must obviously be, up to a point, concurrent in time; and the major poet, with his superior powers of assimilation and the universality of his understanding, can to a considerable extent anticipate the first process. The key-word is 'understanding,' imaginative comprehension: we cannot be said to understand a thing till we have realized it in relation with at least its immediate environment, and the poet cannot arrive at this understanding in advance of the general consciousness of his age.

To take a concrete example. When railways first appeared in England, they were bound to be—and remain for some time—alien to the visual consciousness. Until they ceased to be foreign bodies, until the eye had learnt to accept them with the same ease as it accepted clouds, horses or windmills, the fact of railway could not become integrated with the specific poetic conscious- ness. Tennyson might, if he had chosen, have written a poem describing a train in terms of something else; but he could not be expected to use one metaphorically, to describe something else in terms of a train. But to-day we do not most of us feel, to use a common idiom, that a railway 'spoils the view': we have learnt to understand it in relation to its environment. So the poet is able to use it for metaphor, and we get lines like the fol- lowing which were written originally in an epithalamium:

> Let us be off. Our steam
> Is deafening the dome.
> The needle in the gauge
> Points to a long-banked rage
> And trembles there to show
> What a pressure's below.
> Valve cannot vent the strain
> Nor iron ribs refrain
> That furnace in the heart.
> Come on, make haste and start
> Coupling-rod and wheel,
> Welded of patient steel,
> Piston that will not stir
> Beyond the cylinder
> To take in its stride
> A teeming countryside. . . .
> (C. Day Lewis.)

These lines are quoted only to demonstrate that no oddity need arise through the employment of 'modern' data in verse: they also demonstrate, perhaps, the danger of a modern poet writing pastiche of metaphysical verse in the course of trying to find a solution of the same problem that the metaphysicals tackled. Where his or their metaphor degenerates into a series of isolated and barren conceits, it is a sign that either the general or the poetic consciousness has not sufficiently assimilated its material. (For an example of the railway engine described in terms of something else, the reader is referred to Spender's poem, 'The Express.')

Hopkins is remarkable, amongst other things, for the extent of his vocabulary: no poet since Donne had drawn his material from so wide a radius, though Hopkins drew comparatively little from the specifically modern data which lay to hand. It is in his ordering of words that he is the technical forerunner of the post-war poets, the first 'modern' poet, and a most evident link between them and Donne. And, in spite of lines like—

> ... And when Peace here does house
> He comes with work to do, he does not come to coo,
> He comes to brood and sit.

it is more to the prose-style of the seventeenth-century divines, and particularly to Donne's, that Hopkins links us. The connection is obvious in such a passage as: 'In a flash, at a trumpet crash, I am all at once what Christ is, since He was what I am, and This Jack, joke, poor potsherd, patch, matchwood, immortal diamond, Is immortal diamond.' We have an idea which compels to itself a number of objects within its magnetic field, and these objects are related to each other often through an intensive alliteration and assonance. There follow a few extracts from recent verse. In A we have the mal-digested influence of Hopkins only: in B and C, verse illustrating the properly assimilated, combined influence of Donne and Hopkins, working on the lines sketched out above: in D, an example of Spender's fluid-image technique, which is affiliated to the kind of magnetically-grouped image technique noticed in Donne and Hopkins, without deriving from it.

A

Me, March, you do with your movements master and rock
With wing-whirl, whale-wallow, silent budding of cell. ...

(W. H. Auden.)

B

Crofter, leader of hay, working in sweat and weathers, tin-streamer, heckler, blow-room major, we are within a vein's distance of your prisoned blood. . . .

(W. H. Auden.)

C

The quietude of a soft wind,
Will not rescind
My debts to God but gentle skinned
His finger probes, I lull myself
In quiet in diet in riot in dreams
In dopes in drams in drums in dreams
Till God retire and the door shut.
But
Now I am left in the fire-blaze
The peacefulness of the fire-blaze
Will not erase
My debts to God for his mind strays
Over and under and all ways
All days and always.

(Louis Macneice.)

D

. . . Eye, gazelle, delicate wanderer,
Drinker of horizon's fluid line. . . .

(Stephen Spender.)

Donne and the metaphysicals used the concentration of images and the juxtaposition of paradoxical ideas in such a way as to give the reader a series of intellectual shocks: Hopkins used an intense concentration of images in such a way as to give the reader a series of sensual shocks: when the post-war poet is successful in his use of concentrated images and paradoxically juxtaposed ideas, the effect is generally a dramatic one: this is especially noticeable in Auden's work. There is a perpetual interplay between the surface images and an underlying dramatic situation or series of situations. This is probably the reason why so many recent poems seem to us incomplete, affairs of scattered climaxes and fine lines, rather than self-contained poems: for the strength of the dramatic lies in its manifold implications, while the strength of the lyric lies in the complete statement of a single selected facet of experience. To attempt, as many post-war poets do, to express within a lyric compass the range of a dramatic situation must tend, therefore, to produce poems allusive, over-concentrated and unfinished in effect. It is probably a more or less conscious understanding of this that leads Auden to writing long poems.

Eliot was the first person in England to exploit this dramatic-situation kind of poetry through the medium of 'modern' imagery. 'Prufrock' begins:

> Let us go then, you and I,
> When the evening is spread out against the sky
> Like a patient etherized upon a table. . . .

And in the work of younger poets we constantly come across this interaction between a very wide range of 'modern' imagery, from geology to golf-courses, and a latent dramatic situation which often contains a doubling of psychological and political character. It is not suggested that a poet cannot write poetry to-day without bringing in anæsthetics and machines. If he is excited by a railway engine, well and good: if he is not, let him leave it alone and stop flirting with fashion by faking an emotion. It *is* suggested, however, that a new seam of richest material has been opened up and that poets are learning how to convert that raw material to their own uses. They are only beginning to assimilate the tough ore, but the face of poetry is visibly changing and its future lies in this direction. They are learning to communicate through a new kind of power, like the pylon-carried wires of which Spender writes —

> But far above and far as sight endures
> Like whips of anger
> With lightning's danger
> There runs the quick perspective of the future. . . .

f

CHAPTER X

A CRITIC, writing recently on Auden, Spender and myself, claimed to have found in our work 'the return of the lyrical impulse, banished by Eliot.' It is difficult to understand how a man, even a man of Eliot's authority, can banish an impulse: nor can I accept this idea of lyricism as a sort of tide which can go out and leave all the poets high and dry, then come in again and carry them all off their feet. The lyrical impulse, in so far as that means anything, is present in every poet; it is, when all is said and done, what makes him write poetry rather than prose. There have been no good poets who have not occasionally written lines of pure lyrical quality, and comparatively few who have not occasionally written a lyric. But the true lyric poet is a very rare bird indeed. By 'a true lyric poet,' I mean one who can always write a lyric when he wants to and often does want to. In this class I doubt if one could include, of English poets, more than Shakespeare, a few of the Elizabethans, Herrick, Blake, Tennyson perhaps, and Housman. The pure lyric is, in the first place, more absolutely self-contained and self-sufficient than any other kind of poem. It is, secondly, the nearest approach to music amongst the other arts, not only because of its origin as a form of words sung to music, but also because of its impersonality: the perfect lyric is a poem from which the author has withdrawn once he has set it in motion, and has allowed the dance of words to form its own patterns. Both its mood and its texture must give the appearance of complete smoothness and homogeneousness. Logic, wit, introspection, emotional complexity are alike foreign to it. The lyric, therefore, is a form in which both the impersonality of the material and the un-self-consciousness of the creator are raised to highest power.

If we accept some such definition of the lyric, we shall be bound to look askance at the common contemporary critical dictum that it is very difficult to write lyrics to-day: the answer is that for most poets it always has been. On the other hand we may be free to agree with the critic quoted above to the extent of saying that it is particularly difficult to-day for the *lyrical impulse* to find outlets. In so far as this means something more than that it is particularly difficult to-day to write poetry, and refers specially to the writing of lines or passages of pure lyrical quality, the difficulties may be summed up as follows. First, the trained self-consciousness, which is the best result of modern psychological theory, intervenes between the poet's moods and his poetry: the problem set for him by a given mood, which was once solved by the poem that resulted from the mood, is now apt to be solved by a self-consciousness trained to work on psycho-analytic lines. The poetical motive-power of a mood is diminished, though not destroyed, when that mood has been rationally explained.

There arises from this another point. Behind lyrical poetry we feel always a certain irresponsibility: the lyric is the form of poetry, more than any other, within which the poet is answerable to nothing but its own laws and the experience of his senses. In a state of society where it is unusually difficult for him not to be aware of the large tracts of experience outside his immediate environment and to feel that these demand some attitude from him, as a man, the lyric irresponsibility of the artist is hard to achieve. To put it in another way. Housman, writing of the four eighteenth-century poets in whom he recognizes 'the true poetic accent emerging clearly from the contemporary dialect'—Collins, Smart, Cowper and Blake—says: 'And what other characteristic had these four in common? They were mad.' This madness, the poet's sense of responsibility to nothing but his own inner voice, is perhaps his only way of preserving poetic integrity against the influences of a perverse generation. At the same time, with the wider comprehension of the life and significances of his civilization which the instruments of that civilization give him, the poet to-day is likely to feel that he must needs preserve his own sanity in the teeth of a world gone mad. Madness is a luxury he cannot afford, and a condition the more difficult for him to attain in proportion as he is conscious of its defence-mechanism nature. Where his environment seems to the poet antagonistic and wicked, he will either go mad or turn to didactic writing. Post-war poets have for the most part adopted the second alternative, and consequently we find the lyrical impulse in their work flowing tortuously and with difficulty, often forced underground, carrying a large amount of alluvial deposit with it.

A third and quite different reason for the deficiency of lyrical writing is that the spoken word has been for some time in abeyance. The disappearance of the type of civilization which fostered the minstrel and the ballad-writer, and the decay of poetic drama, had to some degree taken away from the poet the obligation to make his verse musical. Sound is only the surface of lyric, but when the poet has no immediate object in writing for the ear, his verse may cease to present a musical surface. On the other hand, there are signs that poetry is beginning to occupy itself again with the possibilities of sound; and here the wireless should be able to play an important part both in educating the public ear to the spoken word and in providing an opportunity for a new type of poetic drama.

There remains to examine in more detail the technique of post-war poetry, with special reference to its methods of dealing with the lyrical impulse. We have already noticed that short-circuiting of the poetic current which has resulted in the use of image rather than allegory, metaphor rather than simile. In the actual texture of the words we find the same intensification. Spender achieves this by a kind of playing off of one image against another, a technical device akin to the interlacing of themes in music. For instance:

> ... Eye, gazelle, delicate wanderer,
> Drinker of horizon's fluid line. ...

where, instead of the simple definition of one object in terms of another, the orthodox employment of imagery, we have two images of equal value wrestling as it were with one another and bringing out the strength of each. We see it again in his lines:

> ... And who hoarded from the spring branches
> The desires falling across their bodies like blossoms.

Spender is unlike most of his contemporaries in that he relies for poetic effect considerably on the associational value of his words. In his earlier work, at any rate, he proved himself to be a naïf poet and therefore not as conscious as they of the exhaustion under which a great number of words were labouring as a result of having been compelled to represent a multiplicity of poetic associations. Being a true poet, he was able instinctively to limit the associational value of such words and thus to revivify them as poetic agents. The majority of post-war poets, keenly aware of this exhaustion of language, tend to employ words in their denotative rather than their connotative use. The texture of their verse in consequence is apt to be too rigid and uncompromising, a hard concrete surface that gives no resilience, no echo, no sense of depths below. Auden has contrived to avoid this effect in an interesting way. Although in his later work he occasionally exploits the association-value of words after the romantic manner—'Aloof as an admiral on the old rocks,' for instance—he has generally limited their meaning very severely. But the effect of mystery, of untold implications, which the romantics achieved by the juxtaposition of words in such a way as to soften their outlines and make them fuse into each other, Auden achieves by constantly introducing phrases flat and precise on the surface yet suggesting mystery below. Take, for example:

> Nights come bringing the snow, and the dead howl
> Under the headlands in their windy dwelling
> Because the Adversary put too easy questions
> On lonely roads. . . .

In the first two lines 'headlands' and 'windy' derive value from their own connotations, in true romantic style: but in the last two lines every word, even 'lonely' is precise, and the mystery—the poetical meaning—is generated by the phrase as a whole. We find exactly the same thing happening at the lovely end of Poem XVI:

> ... Death of the old gang: would leave them
> In sullen valley where is made no friend,
> The old gang to be forgotten in the spring,
> The hard bitch and the riding master,
> Stiff underground; deep in clear lake
> The lolling bridegroom, beautiful, there.

Here again, the separate words are hard-edged and non-committal as diamonds; it is the dramatic quality and the lively interplay of phrases that achieves the same sort of poetic effect as the Romantics obtained by the marriage of fertile words.

With this pruning of the associational luxuriance of words we may connect a novel use of metaphor which seems likely to become fairly common. Poetical metaphor was originally produced by the changing of the sense of a word from the concrete to the abstract and from the denotative to the connotative. In the course of time this abstract sense became the ordinary meaning of the word and often was exhausted through overwork in poetry. Perceiving this the poet leaves it alone altogether or restores it to life by employing it in a context where the original concrete meaning is stressed and the later metaphorical meaning is either discarded completely or used as an undertone. Thus, one side of a word having become threadbare, it is turned inside out, and what was the simple sense is now the metaphorical one. We see this device in such phrases as:

> ... Just so the pure night-eye, the moon,
> Labours, a monumental mason,
> To *gloss over* a world of stone.

or

> As ocean-flyer clings
> To height, to the last drop of *spirit* driving on. ...

The search for methods for restoring freshness to words con-

tributes to the obscurity of post-war poetry. Poets have gone
back to old grammatical usages and have taken new grammatical
licenses. We notice, for example, the omission of the relative
pronoun and the article, the qualification of nouns by adverbs,
the transposition of the adjective, inversion, and the frequent
employment of elliptic constructions. Where Auden's earlier
poems are obscure, it is due much more often to an elliptic use
of language than to any confusion of the thought or non-con-
ductivity of the images. The reader may be alienated at first by
these licenses, but he will soon find, I think, that they are going
to the construction of an exciting and consistent kind of language with whose idioms practice will quickly make him familiar.
Although Hopkins founded no school, his naïf and successful
experimentation with words entitle him to the position of in-
augurator of this revolution in language: if Eliot, more than
anyone else, is responsible for the new rhythms of verse through
his masterly variations on the iambic line, Hopkins is responsible for the new arrangements and cadences of words.

The emotional complexity to which the modern poet is so
often subject makes sustained lyrical writing very difficult. In
consequence we notice in the verse under examination a constant alternation of lyricism and flatness. This was the method of
the French Symbolists, and it is the salient characteristic of post-
war verse technique. The deliberate insertion into a lyrical context of pieces of slang and 'prosaic' words: the juxtaposition of
highly-charged 'poetical' images and dull, commonplace images,
the use of bathos and of carefully selected banalities; all these
have been taken over from the Symbolists, largely through the
instrumentality of Eliot, and the verse that results offers an un-
even, conversational surface shot through with gleams of lyricism rather than a uniformly lyrical texture. Here are some typical
lines from a poem by Louis MacNeice, 'Sunday Morning':

> Down the road someone is practising scales,
> The notes like little fishes vanish with a wink of tails,
> Man's heart expands to tinker with his car
> For this is Sunday morning. . . .

Just as these poets go back on occasion to old grammatical forms, so they draw frequently upon the older forms of verse technique: we may instance Auden's modified use of the sprung-rhythm and set alliterations found in 'Piers Plowman.' Free verse, if it ever existed outside the heated imagination of reactionary critics and the parlour-games of parodists, can certainly not be said to exist here: even Spender's verse, which uses rhyme very sparingly and generally dispenses with a set metre, is based on an underlying sprung-rhythm. The desire for intensity and for freshness of language which leads these poets to syntactical ellipse, produces also that preoccupation with internal rhyme and assonance which may succeed in re-establishing poetry as a delight for the ear. Owen's alliterative assonance is constantly employed, and many experiments are being made on the lines of Hopkins's internal rhyming and vowel modulation. I myself have written a number of poems on a pattern of cross-assonance: for example—

> *Now* to be with you, elate, *unshared*,
> My *kestrel* joy, O *hoverer* in wind,
> *Over* the quarry furiously at *rest*
> *Chaired* on shoulders of *shouting* wind. ....

Internal and cross rhyming can impart a subdued, sustained melodic tone to verse, and enable the writer to use rhyme words which have grown stale as end-rhymes. Finally it may be said that, while no amount of technical experiment can of itself produce poetry, the fact of such widespread experimentation is some indication of poetry being in a healthy and hopeful state.

CHAPTER XI

IT is easier to describe the effects of poetry than the nature of the poet. We may find, after long research, a formula that will fit the latter: but no form of words has ever been discovered capable of pinning down the nature of poetry. A sprite, a winged joy, it jigs in the air before our eyes, with a moment of brilliance making mortal fields elysian, taking colour from the sun and variety from the earth, gorgeous against thunderclouds, at home also on the rubbish-heap and the railway embankment, evading without effort the net of the logician and the killing-bottle of the psychologist. So it is that, in despair of ever grasping this capricious and untamed flyer, we are driven to define the nature of poetry by its effects upon us.

Emily Dickinson, the American poet, wrote: 'If I read a book and it makes my whole body so cold no fire can ever warm me, I know it is poetry. If I feel physically as if the top of my head were taken off, I know this is poetry. These are the only ways I know it.' Professor Housman in a recent lecture gave evidence of the hair-raising effect poetry has upon him. 'Experience has taught me, when I am shaving of a morning, to keep watch over my thoughts, because, if a line of poetry strays into my memory, my skin bristles so that the razor refuses to act.' I have known several people who share my own sensation on approaching a passage of poetry where that strong enchantment lies in wait — one of suffocation, followed by a sense of physical lightening and relief: the same sensation as one receives, for instance, at the entrance of the celestial motif in Beethoven's A minor quartet, as though the world held its breath waiting for an angel to appear. There can be little doubt that this emotional disturbance in the reader is a reproduction of the disturbance which was the poetical impulse of the writer; and this reproduction is the first aim and effect of poetry. The first test of poetry is an empiric one.

The poet's chief aim, then, is to communicate not the exact

detail of an experience, but its tone and rhythm. There is, however, a secondary effect of poetry. It gives pleasure, the seventeenth-century critics said: it interests us, we should say to-day.
We may be insensitive to the first effect of a poem, its pure communication, yet be interested by something else in it. As Housman has pointed out: 'Poems very seldom consist of poetry and
nothing else; and pleasure can be derived from their other ingredients.' (In the last chapter I proposed the hypothesis that a
pure poetry exists, employing the term 'lyric' to describe poems
which 'consist of poetry and nothing else.') We have also suggested that a great deal of the comparative popularity of the
post-war writers with whom I have been dealing is due to an
interest in other ingredients of their verse—its political significance, for example, or its contemporary colouring—rather than
to a perception of whatever 'pure' poetry there may be in it. At
the same time, we must not undervalue this interest: a book
which aims to attract people towards post-war verse is justified
in stressing the pleasure which such verse can give, and it is to
be hoped that its claim to possess a real and special interest of
its own has been established by the extracts already given. It is
also the experience of the present writer that several of the post-
war poets are not deficient in the capacity to produce 'pure'
poetry. Just as I am unable to agree with those critics who so
ingeniously and sometimes so unscrupulously seek to prove
that modernist verse has no meaning, for the simple reason that
I cannot avoid understanding many poems which they have
pronounced unintelligible; so, when other critics assert that
there is not enough poetry in post-war verse to raise one hair
upon them and make them catch a single breath; I can only say
that I am sorry but I have found it otherwise. If they care to
claim universality for their own indifference and to presume that
where they have had no visitation, there can be no angels present, I should not wish to make an equal counterclaim and de-
clare that my excitement in reading some poems of Spender and
Auden is the final verdict on their poetry. Let each reader decide

for himself. Time will count the votes and announce the win-
ners.

The effects of poetry are to reproduce a state of mind, or to
cause interest and pleasure, or both. What is the nature of the
poet? Here again there is no way to speak but in parable. A wireless station: masts rooted in earth, stretching towards heaven,
sensitive to the horizontal waves of sound: an instrument recep-
tive of the messages that crowd the air: another instrument,
translating these messages out of code into a universal language,
selecting and co-ordinating them, transmitting them to whoso-
ever will turn a dial. The poet listens in to his universe. His
senses are the filaments which conduct experience into the instrument of his imagination. That instrument's range of recep-
tivity is one measure of his greatness as a poet. It is an instrument which all men possess, but with the poet it is specially
adapted so as to catch the potentially poetic significances of his
experience and to pass them on to the second instrument
through a kind of poetic filter. The second instrument is the
conscious process by which the filtered stream of experience is
directed into a poem, the process we call technique: his ability in
conducting this process is the second measure of a poet's greatness.

It is the nature of the poetic vision to perceive those invisible
truths which are like electrons the basis of reality; the nature of
the poetic imagination to become aware of the cryptic links that
bind our universe together, to find similarity in difference and
to make coherence out of contradiction. If the poet is not clairvoyant, he is nothing. And this clairvoyancy is particularly
directed towards discovering the 'supernatural' in nature and the
'superhuman' in humanity. There can be no such thing as realist
poetry. The landscape, the city street painted by the poet is not
the landscape or the street that we know: the hills to which he
lifts up his eyes are not marked on any map. Helen and Hector,
Oedipus, Lear, Iago, Captain Ahab—there has never been a
creature of the poetic imagination that was not more than

human. Even in prose fiction the characters that stand out are those that both contain and transcend humanity. The poet makes timeless legends out of our mortal, savage dust; and he can also give blood and bones to a myth.

I believe that this clairvoyant power is to be found here and there in post-war poetry. Auden in particular has an astonishing eye for seeing sermons in stones. As we read his work we are constantly, as in the work of Rilke, coming across this poetical animation of inanimate objects, and he discovers poetry in the most unlikely places and wrings it out of the most recalcitrant material. For the century has brought us not only new things to see but new ways of seeing: and Auden's poetry gives us, as all good poetry does, an original angle of vision.

> Consider this and in our time
> As the hawk sees it or the helmeted airman. . . .

Auden's, vision, when he is at his best, combines the minute, concentrated seeing of the hawk and the broad panorama of the airman, and it contains something of the passionless objectivity of both. Again, the mythopoieic faculty which we have claimed as one of poetry's greater powers, is evident in post-war verse. It is at work in the ancestor-worship we have already noticed, creating and drawing energy from the superhuman. We find it in the symbolic characters that raise their heads so often in these poems: Warner's engineer, 'Colonel Humphries'; Auden's 'Captain Ferguson' or his 'Gerhart Meyer from the sea, the truly strong man.' We do not suggest that these characters are immortal, but they are vivid and illuminating; they represent something essential in humanity magnified to heroic proportions; and they may be the forerunners of a new Achilles, a new Job, a new Othello.

The poet is an artificer by profession, an architect experimenting with a variety of materials, concerned with levels and stresses, old foundations, new designs. Then suddenly, perhaps in one window only in the last of many houses he has built, a light shows. An unearthly visitor has taken up possession, the pure spirit of poetry. The works of great poets blaze with light from every storey. But one single window so illuminated can justify a life's work, while a thousand structures of graceful design are vain and void without that fiery occupant. The poet is an artificer by profession, a poet by divine accident. The pure spirit that comes to possess him, for one minute may be in twenty years, comes from regions over which he has no control. Between visits there is nothing he can do but work at his profession, so that, when next an angel arrives, he can better accommodate him. He may hope, but he cannot be certain, that the finer the tenement the more likely it is to be tenanted.

That is as much as we can ever know of the nature of poetry — the angel seen at the window, the air of glory. Whence these visitors come the poet cannot say: whether out of the upper air, influences from the source of all light: or are daimons, the lords of energy, alive in all matter: or from the dark continent in his own mind where mankind's past is stored, an Atlantis lost beneath the waves of consciousness. If this last is so, if the pure breath of poetry is an emanation from the primitive forms of life preserved in the strata of his soul, then we might predict that the gradual extension of self-consciousness will after many centuries be the death of poetry. We might think of the region whence these voices come as a native reserve inch by inch absorbed by the encroachment of civilization. Yet if a thousand years is to the poet but as yesterday, his to-morrow has a like span to run. That is a hope for poetry. The voices are vigorous still, not dead. We hear them when Spender writes —

> Also the swallows by autumnal instinct
> Comfort us with their effortless exhaustion
> In great unguided flight to their complete South. . . .

or,

The valley with its gilt and evening look
And the green chestnut
Of customary root
Are mocked dry like the parched bed of a brook...

Some claim that they are to be heard in the verse of MacNeice and Madge. They are strongest, to my mind, in those lines where Auden fights free of self-consciousness, æsthetic theorizing and contemporary despair. In —

There are some birds in these valleys
Who flutter round the careless
With intimate appeal,
By seeming kindness trained to snaring,
They feel no falseness. . . .
. . . Alas, the signal given,
Fingers on trigger tighten.
The real unlucky dove
Must smarting fall away from brightness
Its love from living.

or,

The two worlds in each other's arms,
Falcon is poised over fell in the cool,
Salmon draws
Its lovely quarrons through the pool.
A birthday, a birth
On English earth
Restores, restore will, has restored
To England's story
The directed calm, the actual glory.

Nigel Curtis Raleigh.

dd. Patricia.

Nov: 8th. 1934.